SUE YOUR BANK

How to

Fight Back

with **Little or No Money,**

Make Sense of Your

H.A.M.P. Nightmare,

& **Take Back**

Your Life!

By Alan R. Sims

Alan R. Sims

Sue Your Bank

First Edition July 2012

Amended February 2013

Alan R. Sims

Courtroom Advocates

101 E. Redlands Blvd./Suite 215-E

Redlands, CA 92373

Printed in the United States of America

Alan R. Sims

"If a million consumers filed a million small claims court actions a year against the banks, the banks would either try to abolish the small claims court or improve their performance."

-Ralph Nader

Alan R. Sims

Dedication

This book is dedicated to **American homeowners** who are caught in a H.A.M.P. (Home Affordable Modification Program) nightmare. It is my hope that this book will offer you answers in how to fight back. While fighting back may not pay you back entirely for all that you have suffered, may it give you the hope and strength to move forward in your life.

This book is dedicated to homeowner Dave Graham[1] who trusted me and the organization I formed CLCREE[2] to help homeowners just like him. Thank you for beleiving in my skills to help you fight back. Also thank you for agreeing to tell your story in our hometown newspaper as well as on national television in hopes of helping others. Together we accomplished the first victory of its kind in proving fraud against a Goliath Bank and lived a true David vs. Goliath story. Your story has inspired many, including me.

---

[1] See http://youtu.be/BVO_o_tNzJI or search "Sue Your Bank: How To Sue a Bank for Fraud or www.SueYourBank.com/video

[2] CLCREE (The Center for Litigation & Consumer Real Estate Education) has since been changed to Courtroom Advocates (www.Courtroom-Advocates.com

To **John Wells** of Channel 6 Big Bear for being the first to invite me on his local television show to broadcast my mission. At that time (2008) the housing crisis was in its infancy and few were feeling its affects. Many homeowners were not ready to receive my message. It was John who had faith in me to get this important message out and empower his audience.

To the **Big Bear Grizzly Newspaper** Big Bear Lake, CA for telling our story in great detail and for giving my neighbors hope to fight back. I would especially like to thank journalist **Arrissia Owen Turner** for the detailed local coverage.

To **Dylan Ratigan** of **The Dylan Ratigan Show on MSNBC** and **his producers**: Thank you for allowing Dave Graham to tell his story and for putting a national spotlight on our message. Your coverage of the "Fraudclosure" crisis provided many homeowners with much needed answers. Sadly, Mr. Ratigan left MSNBC in June of 2012.

However, he has a lot of brilliant insights on the foreclosure crisis and I encourage readers of this book to follow him on his website, Dylan Ratigan.com. He has just released a book called ***Greedy Bastards***.

This book is dedicated to my wife, **Cathleen** for her support and sacrifice as we built this organization. I could not have written this book without you! I love you!

Alan R. Sims

Disclaimer

The writer of this book **is not** an attorney. This book discusses and explains general legal information and **does not constitute legal <u>advice</u> in any respect.** If you want assurance that the legal information is appropriate for your individual situation, the author urges you to consult an attorney. This book outlines the author's successes but in **no way should be construed as a guarantee** that you will be successful. Individual circumstances, level of preparation, case building, and judges will vary.

Alan R. Sims

Foreward

As American homeowners battle losing their homes due to the fraudulent greedy acts of banks, the government sits back and does nothing!

As an attorney who has filed numerous lawsuits against banks, I have seen firsthand the tragedies the banks have caused American families and the economy as a whole. Using H.A.M.P., the banks seduce homeowners into a loan modification with the promise to lower monthly mortgage payments, lower interest rates and to reduce the principle of their loan. The fact is, the bank will eventually foreclose on their home and receive multiple government benefits to do so!

I have met only one man with the passion, education, and experience to bring light to the fraud and misrepresentation of the banks. Alan R. Sims is a pioneer in his field and an expert witness I have hired on numerous occasions throughout my legal career. He realized early on the average homeowner cannot afford full blown litigation in our courts today.

With the cost of court expenses and rising attorney fees, these lawsuits are highly cost prohibitive for many. Alan has been assisting homeowners understand the issues they are facing against the banks. Through his assistance, he has helped the American homeowner have their day in court.

This book is backed by Mr. Sims' experiences as an expert witness in small claims and higher courts and the benefits his clients have achieved without the need of a lawyer or a law degree. He shows there is justice for all through the court system and educates the American homeowner with information that is elusive to so many.

-Goldy M. Berger, Esquire[3]

---

[3] The Law Offices of Goldy M. Berger.
www.LawOfficesOfGoldyBerger.com

Table of Contents

Is This Book for You?

My name is Alan Sims. I have a passion for problem solving in all matters of real estate. I have spent thousands of hours over many years researching workable, affordable answers to empower the American homeowner to fight back. I have fought complex mortgage scam organizations and banks of all shapes and sizes. I know what works and what does not.

This book offers an easy-to-follow format on how to sue a bank, *why* you would want to, and how to do it without going broke, without wasting years in legal limbo, and how to restore your credit all for little or no money.

The focus of this book is suing in *small claims court* to offer affordable solutions to the millions of homeowners who are low on finances and options. However, as a court approved expert witness, I have worked with attorneys offering these theories in *higher courts* as well.

If you are reading this book in an effort to save your home from foreclosure, this book <u>is not for you</u>. The truth is, if you are unable to pay your mortgage it is *very* *likely* that your home will go into foreclosure eventually.

I am known for my forthright, frank personality. If you have not heard the above statement before, and have spent thousands of dollars to fix this impossible situation and searched for, and believed *anyone* who has promised you they will save your home, you will *not* find that answer in *this* book. There will be other "truths" in this book that you may have not heard before. My mission is to arm you with this truth so you can make informed decisions in your life and fight back with this information. What *you will find*, is an approach that can work if you are willing to invest the time in learning something new, be open minded, and have the heart to fight back. What you may get at the end is <u>some money</u> in your pocket and possibly your credit restored to what it was before this "odyssey" began.

This book does not come with a guarantee. I *cannot* guarantee any outcome. The large part of the job to prove you were wronged will be on you - "the burden of proof." Anytime you bring a lawsuit against another party it is *up to you* to prove your case. This book first serves to educate you and help you decide if it is worth the fight.

Secondly, once you decide, this book will arm you with how to go about it.

The purpose of this book is to help you rebuild your life if you have (a) already lost your home; or, (b) are involved in H.A.M.P. right now and are getting no where; or, (c) you feel you may lose your home despite trying to modify your mortgage in any loan modification program.

I am not a lawyer so please don't look for actual legal advice. This book contains legal information. Lawyers rely on my *information* to help them make their case (which I will explain later), however, by law I cannot give you legal advice.

I wrote this book to provide an affordable solution to fight your bank. While there are many books out there on small claims court and how to represent yourself in all courts, there are few experts who have successfully sued and want to share their "recipe" for how they did it. I wrote this book to provide you with an affordable solution.

As you read on, you will discover ways to pursue a lawsuit that will cost you little or no money-depending on your personal financial circumstance and where you live (your jurisdiction).

I also wrote this book because the banks and mortgage scammers are *counting* on the fact that you will not have enough money to fight back. They are also counting on you not having the heart or the energy to fight back. For this reason, I hope when you read this book it makes you **mad!** When you're mad, you're motivated-motivated to take action and move forward with your life. For those who desire to take action, this book is for you.

A Typical Day at the Office

When a potential new client comes into my office our conversation starts something like this:

<u>Sims:</u> "Why do you want to sue your bank?"

Client: "They didn't give me a loan modification and because of this, I (a) will lose my home, or (b) have already lost my home."

<u>Sims:</u> "You can't sue your bank just because they didn't give you a loan modification. They don't *have to* give you one. It's voluntary. You need to tell me more. Did the bank promise you anything?"

Client: "They told me (a) I had to stop paying my mortgage, or, (b) I had to start with a trial modification program."

<u>Sims:</u> "Did the bank tell you that after a trial program-say after 3 months or so, that you would get a loan modification?"

Client: "Yes!"

****

Now you have the basis of a lawsuit. Why? Because they promised you something, you relied on that promise, and you paid them money in exchange for that promise. You gave them money (made mortgage payments) because they promised you something. This forms the basis of a simple contract.

An enforceable contract is not just that someone offers you something and you receive it. In order for a contract to be an enforceable one, money (also called "consideration" in the legal field) needs to be involved.

Here are some examples of a contract in your daily life:

1.) You go into a diner and they offer you coffee. It is understood that in exchange for that coffee the diner will receive money. For a contract, there has to be an offer ("Would ya like some coffee?"). There has to be acceptance ("I'd love some!"). There has to be money exchanged for the coffee (consideration).

2.) When you drive in to a gas station that promises to have gas, it is understood that to receive some gas, you will pay money.

3.) When the book seller offered you this book, it was understood that in exchange for this book, you would pay money.

Let's add a further layer of explanation as to why you have a case against the bank. You will not just argue that you had a contract and that contract was broken. You will argue that you *relied* on that promise *and* you relied on it to your detriment. This concept is called detrimental reliance.[4]

Had you **not** relied on that promise, you would have made plans for your future. Had you known that this promise was never going to be fulfilled, you could have walked away from this home and not had your credit ruined. Instead, you were paying a reduced mortgage payment for a trial period that is *supposed* to be 3 months (according to H.A.M.P. guidelines) but was stretched out for over a year *or more*. You *relied* on what the bank *promised* in hopes of continuing to live in your home.

---

[4] Detrimental Reliance: Reliance by one party on the acts or representations of another, causing a worsening of the first party's position. Detrimental reliance may serve as a substitute for consideration (exchange of money) and thus make a promise enforceable as a contract. See promissory estoppel. (from Black's Law Dictionary).

In one of my organization's first court victories against a huge bank you will learn how I helped a homeowner fight back by arguing exactly this point. As you read through this book you will learn how you can argue this point too-with or without my assistance.

You will also learn things that may shock you as you traveled through this experience. In the MSNBC interview[5] you will hear about 2 minutes into the interview, that the payments Dave made never actually went towards his mortgage. They were placed in an account to pay property taxes and insurance on the house so that the bank could subsidize what would eventually become *their* house. Later on in this book, I will go over the points made in the MSNBC interview in line-by-line detail to help you fully understand.

The legal term related to the exchange between you and the bank is called promissory estoppel (it can also incorrectly be called *equitable estoppel*).

(1) A bank employee promises you something (that ends up not being true) and

---

[5] See http://youtu.be/BVO_o_tNzJI or search "Sue Your Bank: How To Sue a Bank for Fraud or www.SueYourBank.com/video

(2) you rely on that promise in good faith, and

(3) it becomes a disadvantage to you later because you lose your home and the bank comes out of the agreement ending up with *your* money and *your* house!

Explained in a more scholarly, lawyerly way: *In contract law, promissory estoppel applies if the actions a party has undertaken by the offeree* (the homeowner) *while under contract would be unfairly detrimental to the interests of the offeree* (the homeowner) *and would unjustly enrich the offeror* (the bank). *As a general legal principle, estoppel* (which really means "stop") *is meant to halt any action which would be unfair to the interests of one party in comparison to another.*

To repeat my point: if the bank had *not* promised you a loan modification, you would have said, "Well, Mr. Bank, I can't pay my mortgage," and you would have walked away from the home, sold it, put if up for a short sale, let it go into foreclosure, etc. Your life would have gone on and you would have also gone on with that money in your pocket (instead of the bank's pocket). But because you relied on this promise, you kept paying (at a financial detriment to you) only to find out regardless of the promise, you lost your home.

Furthermore, you should know that once the bank starts you in a trial period with H.A.M.P. they don't warn you that your credit will be affected. By not warning you the bank has essentially robbed you of options to move forward with your life. By now having a poorer credit score, it is more difficult to rent an apartment, find other options to refinance your home and possibly find a decent job.

So what if the bank representative argued back, "I never said that!?" The proof is, they *did say it* because you paid money (consideration) at an amount that the bank dictated. *That is your proof.* I say this because I read so many advice columns that discourage homeowners by saying, "It will be your word against the banks." While technically true, why would you have paid a certain amount of money for a year and a half? _And_-why would the bank accept that payment, for a year and a half, without complaint? Did you just pick a number and start paying? No! You paid what they told you to pay.

Start thinking about how you would explain what happened in your individual situation while applying these concepts. While no one, most importantly, the judge will have expected that you have gone to law school, what he[6] *will* expect is that you understand the legal concept that you are arguing (we will go into this in more detail further on in this book). Start trying to understand the concepts. See if you can effortlessly explain it to a friend (without referring to notes) and prove that you know it by citing an example (preferably your own personal situation with your bank).

****

So let's get back to the conversation I am having with the potential new client at our "typical day at the office:"

Sims: "So the bank kept advising you to continue sending your money and would eventually give you an answer that you were approved for the loan modification?"

Client: "Yes!"

---

[6] *Please bear with me-I realize there are female judges. I thought it a better use of time and space to stick with one gender than to say "he or she" throughout this book. The use of the word "he" when referring to judges is not meant to offend or exclude anyone.*

<u>Sims</u>: "This is where most people start feeling the "pinch" of that promise they relied on. They eventually start receiving notices from their credit card companies adjusting their credit *down*. This is because the bank has reported the homeowner as making late payments. Imagine if you had a crystal ball-and you knew that they *would not* have given you a loan modification-despite their promises-and you would have lost your home. Would you have applied for a loan modification in the first place?"

****

Now we're looking at "damages." In the legal world damages is another word for money. When you think of damage, think in terms of how much you lost monetarily speaking. We will talk about other things you may have lost such as your health, possibly your marriage and if it's wise to claim those as "damages" as well.

****

So continuing on at our "typical day at the office:"

<u>Sims</u>: "So the bank said essentially, 'You pay us $X.00 for the next three months on a trial loan modification and you will get a

permanent loan modification.' Is that what happened?"

Client: "Yes!"

Sims: "So here it is 18 months (or more) later. You kept paying based on their promise all in hopes of holding on to your home."

Alan R. Sims

Who Am I and What Do I Know?

I am not a lawyer. I teach them, I work with them, I advise them but I am not one. I am an expert witness.

What does that mean? If you have watched a Hollywood movie or television show featuring a legal drama, you may be lead to believe it is the lawyer who will conduct an investigation, solve the crime (or civil matter), and testify to whatever the issue is. The "Hollywood" lawyer will solve the legal issue in 30 minutes to 2 hours.

In reality, in the legal field, it is the expert witness who identifies your issue, does a forensic analysis by going back and reconstructing events, applying legal strategies to solve your dispute, and then testifies to it (if it goes to trial)-all while working with your lawyer. It takes months, sometimes years of digging to gather all the intricate pieces of "the puzzle." One piece out of place and the puzzle picture weakens and the case is not as strong. It is a tremendous responsibility, as well as a privilege to be entrusted in this way. Many of the people I work for will invest substantial amounts of money and heavily rely on me. Literally, the wealth they have worked their entire life building can be riding on my advice and insights. In the scope of one's lifetime, it can sometimes be one of the battles of a person's life.

I equate being an expert witness with being an anesthesiologist-the doctor who puts you to sleep when you have an operation. *Stay with me* and you'll get the point.

You may want a facelift. You may find the absolute best plastic surgeon to do this and pay top dollar for it. In actuality, when you are on the operating room table, it is the anesthesiologist who has the most important job in protecting your health *and your life*.

When you are under anesthesia, it is *this* expert who is watching your blood pressure second-to-second, and depending on the type of anesthesia used, actually *breathes* for you.

The plastic surgeon is working away to give you a (hopefully) beautiful result but it is the anesthesia expert who will make sure you come out of this alive. They don't *guarantee* you will come out alive, but in the majority of cases, they do everything to see that you do. There is also *no guarantee* that you will come out of the surgery beautiful, let alone healthy, however the two work together to try to give you the best result.

What is ironic is that few people will ever speak to the anesthesiologist for very long, if at all. They usually won't ask if they are the best at what they do. The patient actually knows little about them-yet they have the highly important role to keep you alive. In the scope of one's lifetime, it can sometimes be one of the battles of the patient's life as they lay on the operating room table and entrust others with this very important outcome.

The same thing happens in the legal field, the lawyer and the expert witness work together and do the best they can to give you a positive result but the lawyer gets the credit in the Hollywood story and usually in life.

While it is not my role to keep you alive, like the anesthesia expert, little is known about me and what I do. When was the last time you heard of a person searching for the best expert witness? When was the last time you saw a news conference after a famous trial and the expert spoke? Sure, it happens sometimes-but not very often. Don't misunderstand me-I have no problem working behind the scenes. I do hope that next time, however, if you do have to hire a lawyer for any reason, that you find out more about your experts.

So how did this become my career? It all started almost 20 years ago, when I was working as an engineer and the economy (the *last* bad economy) forced me to explore other career options as corporate America was "downsizing." As the economy changed in the 1990s, it was inevitable my career had to change as well.

I embarked on a 7 year apprentice program to become a *commercial* real estate appraiser. I built on my engineering knowledge to work in real estate disputes and fight cases involving construction, etc.

Many people who are not in the real estate field do not realize that there are different levels of appraisers. Your personal experience is that someone comes to your home, maybe takes measurements, photos, and fills in a form. In my role, I appraise sky scrapers, casinos, large estates, etc.

As this present economic situation was developing, I expanded my role to include examining mortgage and real estate fraud. Long before you were personally feeling the effects of the collapsing real estate market, I was examining and projecting what would happen, and sadly, what *did* happen. As the situation progressed, I could see that this collapse was going to be different and would be massive and far-reaching. As you can now see, it has affected the entire world.

The scope of this book is not to re-tell how this happened to you in great detail, but if you are curious, I recommend reading *The Housing Boom and Bust* by Thomas Sowell. While written by a famous economist, it is written in a riveting, very easy to read style-*almost* like a novel. If you want a true understanding of how this happened and apply it to your world, I highly recommend this book. It will probably surprise you to know that this phenomenon has been in the making for quite sometime.

As a mortgage fraud expert, I grew frustrated as I saw my neighbors losing their homes. I formed a non-profit to do something to help. I helped many, but as the economy worsened, few homeowners could afford my services. In the majority of cases, they came to me after they had spent several thousands of dollars on so-called experts who promised them they could save their home-only to be taken for a long, painful, and expensive ride. Also, many tried to hire an attorney (also costing thousands) who assured them they could save their home. Perhaps this happened to you.

I did not have a large advertising budget. I was funding this nonprofit out of my own pocket and did not rely on government funds. I had *some* publicity but it was in small town newspapers so you may have never heard of me. You could possibly find me on the Internet, however, with all the "noise" of people offering you help and empty promises, my services were very hard to find. At the time of publishing this book, I am still hard to find.

So what did I accomplish that was so special and unique and would make me want to write a book about it? I went to small claims court with a local homeowner and friend Dave Graham. In an amazing victory, Dave and I were the first to prove fraud against a large bank-Bank of America. It was the first victory of its kind. The reason you probably never heard of it is victories in small claims court do not make front page news-plain and simple. In fact, in the majority of cases, small claims cases do not make legal precedents that change lives and laws. You just don't hear about them, so you probably heard very little about what Dave and I accomplished.

Before you say to yourself, "Small claims-isn't that where you win just a few thousand dollars?" Bear with me and let me explain how and why Dave chose this option- and how it could benefit you. I ask you to read on and be open minded. I think what you read may surprise you.

Anyway, we assumed that news outlets would *love* to tell a positive David vs. Goliath story to encourage, empower, and inform homeowners-especially in this devastating economy when so few solutions are available. The only large news outlet that wanted to tell our story was Dylan Ratigan on MSNBC.[7]

---

[7] See http://youtu.be/BVO_o_tNzJI or search "Sue Your Bank: How To Sue a Bank for Fraud" or www.SueYourBank.com/video.

Alan R. Sims

Is This Your Story?

As you read on, you will read about Dave Graham and exactly how he won his fight against Bank of America. You will even see the actual court transcript so you can read how *your* fight can be handled.

So who is Dave and why should you care? Dave's story, if you are (or were) involved in the H.A.M.P. program is most likely identical to yours (or very similar). It is also similar to our potential new client at my "typical day at the office" scenario.

In the early part of the Obama administration, H.A.M.P. was introduced as a way to further help American homeowners who were struggling to pay their mortgage. It was a 75 billion dollar program designed to fight the foreclosure crisis. If you read about it in the media you will find that most economic professionals deem it as a dismal failure because it has helped very few. I do not point this out to slam one political party over another. In fact, if you choose to read economist Thomas Sowell's book, you will see that there is plenty of blame to go around on both sides-and has been plenty of blame to go around for decades in regard to the making of this present economic situation.

Whether you just bought your home during the housing "boom" at top dollar or were re-financing a house you've owned for years, your issues with your mortgage occurred because you were placed in a bad mortgage-plain and simple. The reasons why you were placed in a bad mortgage are complex and not easy to explain. However, that's why you were likely placed in a trial period of H.A.M.P.-to repair a bad situation.

Let's revisit why your mortgage was bad. There are many reasons. One that I am professionally familiar with is this: As you went through the loan process an appraiser was sent to appraise your home. In almost every case, the appraiser was being paid by the bank (or mortgage broker). The appraiser, being hungry for work, did whatever the bank said. If the bank said, "Mr. Appraiser, we need you to value the home at exactly $X.00 so we can make this loan work," the appraiser complied. "If you don't appraise the home at this value, we will never hire you again," was the underlying message from the bank. Being an appraiser myself, my office has an estimated 5 inch stack of request forms saying this and more. See my 2009 media coverage on my organization's website in the story featured in South Coast Magazine and you will see what I mean.[8]

The majority of appraisers felt pressured and they succumbed to the bank's demands-that was, if they ever wanted to work again. So behind the scenes, the appraised value of your home was artificially inflated.

When you received the high appraised value, it probably made you happy. The higher the appraised value, the more money you could get in the form of a loan. I'm not blaming you if you felt this way. It's human nature. This is your "castle" so of course you think it is worth a lot. As I said, read the Thomas Sowell book to find out about this practice and more.

As our new president was getting comfortable in his oval office, *your* life was changing because of this economy. You either wanted to take advantage of H.A.M.P. or your bank was strongly suggesting it. *Why would they suggest it?* Because, even though the bank's voluntarily entered into H.A.M.P., they were receiving money from the Federal government if they offered H.A.M.P. to you-even if it was found that eventually you had no chance of ever being approved.

---

[8] www.Courtroom-Advocates.com/media

As I said, life was changing for you. Perhaps you (fill in the blank)_____:

- lost your job;

- you, or a member of your family, had a health crisis;

- had to take care of an aging parent or sick child;

- were about to retire;

- were forced to retire;

- your business went "*bust;*"

- were going through a divorce...

...or a myriad of other life changes we all find ourselves in. It usually does seem to happen at the most inopportune time- "when it rains it pours." Perhaps you were even minding your own business, *paying your mortgage just fine,* when your bank contacted you and suggested a loan modification. Most people would jump at the chance to pay less each month on their mortgage and have some financial "*breathing room.*"

As the months went by, something *weird* started happening to your credit. It may have seemed quite unbelievable at first because you were paying the exact amount the bank told you to pay. Despite this, you began receiving notices from your credit cards that your interest rate was rising or that your credit card(s) was no longer available to you.

As of this publication, banks have foreclosed on more than 4 million homes since the housing crisis began in 2007. There are almost 6 million homes still in danger of foreclosure meaning that 2012 may be the worst year yet for the American homeowner. Though not everyone will face foreclosure, the phenomenon does affect everyone. Homeowners and non-homeowners everywhere will feel a ripple affect on their communities.

Also sadly, if you are like many, you are having a hard time believing that this could happen in America. You may have wondered why there are no solutions to repair this impossible situation. You may have been completely wiped out financially. Out of desperation, you may have even paid so called professionals (including attorneys) who claimed they could save your home. You may have even tried to fight back using other arguments such as "Who owns the note."

While the majority of attorneys have a passion to help you, there are some who will gladly take a several thousand dollar retainer (to start) to try many of these unproven, or barely proven, theories in the legal system. Attorneys that are trying to argue that since "no one knows who owns your mortgage, you can live in the house free and clear," are selling you a pipe-dream. Some cases have been successful but their circumstances are not usual.

In the state of California, where I do most of my work, the state bar is currently chasing after 7,000 bad attorneys all because of the mortgage mess. There are more than that-7,000 is the number because of homeowners who reported them to the state bar. This does not count the attorneys who got away with it because the homeowner was too emotionally beaten down or too embarrassed to speak up.

The state bar is in the same financial crunch that the rest of the world is in. They are not able to hire adequate staff to go after all 7,000+. When they do try each case, the result is that the attorney can no longer practice. That is it. It is very unlikely, that the families who were wronged will be compensated, nor will the families see the several thousand dollars they paid this attorney. The state bar is there to police their own profession-not to save your individual home or solve your problems.

The same is true of the attorney general, the Federal Trade Commission, the F.B.I. mortgage fraud unit, and other organizations. If you read any of their websites carefully, while they would like you to report scams you have been a victim of (*and you should report them*), their resources will be spent to go after the scammer-not to make you whole again. However, if you don't report them, they are free to prey on others and our system and society remain the same.

I told you I am known for my forthright personality so I hope you won't mind if I tell you something that will sting and/or infuriate you: no matter who owns the note or what credentials people have to tell you how they can save you-if you cannot pay your mortgage you will come to learn that you cannot stay in your home.

In an ideal world, what is morally right, or the fact that you are trying hard, worked hard your whole life or any other thing you want to tell yourself to rationalize this impossible, desperate situation-you cannot own a home unless you can pay for it. You may be asking, "*So if it's as bottom line and cut and dried as all that, shouldn't I just stop now? With no home, or losing my home, what else is there to fight about?*" For those of you that believe there is life after this nightmare and do wish to move forward, I ask you to summon your will to fight and read on.

Having said that, I am <u>not</u> asking you to give up. As I stated in the beginning-I am not going to tell you how to save your house, *however,* I am not advising you to give up and do nothing. I am going to tell you how to get *some* money back and restore your credit. Without good, or even fair credit, moving forward will be near impossible. Try finding a job, renting an apartment, or buying the comforts of life without it.

Not yet convinced? Read on and learn more.

Dave's Story

Dave had a very modest home in my neighborhood of Big Bear, California. A lot of love, improvement, and money went into the small home and it was where Dave dreamed of settling down and retiring very soon.

I knew Dave personally and often heard him counting the days until retirement. He was looking forward to settling into this home and eventually enjoying his free time.

Like most Americans, he had a mortgage-and while he was working he had absolutely no problem paying it. However, he knew that eventually, with retirement fast approaching he would have to modify, or lower his mortgage payments.

As luck would have it (or so he thought), he received a phone call from his bank offering to do just that-lower his mortgage payments.

Unbeknownst to Dave, who was not an economist, real estate expert, or banking professional, there was a shift behind the scenes. There was talk of the economy failing, but Dave didn't really feel it yet-however, the Federal government was getting ready for it. The feds were putting pressure on banks (particularly large banks) to "voluntarily" be part of H.A.M.P. (Home Affordable Modification Program). The feds would pay a fee of several thousand dollars to the bank for *each* homeowner they helped in H.A.M.P. The more loans the bank could modify under H.A.M.P., the more fees they would receive from the federal government (i.e., the taxpayers). In order for the bank to get these fees, they had to market to homeowners like Dave.

Dave felt the universe must be a mind-reader and in perfect alignment with his retirement plans. Dave jumped at the chance to get his monthly mortgage payments reduced so his upcoming retirement could be that much more enjoyable.

Another issue that was unbeknownst to Dave: Under H.A.M.P., the bank was supposed to apply a simple mathematical formula-the 31% percent rule. [9] Also, under H.A.M.P. rules, Dave was supposed to get an answer, one way or the other, that he qualified for H.A.M.P. in 3 months (see

---

[9] Payment Reduction Estimator: http://www.makinghomeaffordable.gov/get-assistance/payment-reduction/Pages/default.aspx

question 8 on the link[10]). Dave was thrilled at the chance!

Eagerly, Dave did what he was told because he wanted so badly to qualify for this program. The first thing he was told was that he would be given "trial payments." This meant he would pay several hundred dollars less each month than he had been paying for his home for all those years. Dave was happy to do this, and also to have some financial "breathing room."

The second thing Dave was asked to do was gather many documents that the bank required and send them in. Dave knew how important these documents were to getting approved, so he sent them with a tracking number to know the bank received them.

Another thing that gave Dave reassurance was that he could pay his mortgage over the phone. This gave Dave comfort, because each month he could talk to a "real human" at his bank and ask about his status in H.A.M.P. While on the phone, he would also ask if the bank had received his paperwork. The answer would be, "No."

---

[10] http://www.makinghomeaffordable.gov/get-assistance/explore-eligibility/Documents/HAMP%20for%20Homeowners%20in%20Bankruptcy%20FAQs%20(English).pdf

Even though Dave was armed with tracking numbers, photocopies, etc. the bank would ask him to send it again-3 times in fact. Dave still so badly wanted to qualify that he dutifully followed instructions, and sent it in again.

As a side note, the reason the banks asked Dave to re-send the documents is because they were "buying time." The more time that went by, the longer the bank could prolong the "trial period." With the trial period prolonged, the bank could collect Dave's payments and place them in an escrow account. Unbeknownst to Dave, *the payments he was sending in were **not** paying for his mortgage.* The payments were being kept in an account to pay property taxes and insurance on what eventually would become the bank's property.

Life was continuing for Dave as the months ticked by. Unfortunately something, well, unfortunate was happening to Dave's credit. He was receiving notices, first from his credit card companies that his interest rate was increasing significantly-meaning he now owed more on his credit cards.

He then got news that his credit score was plummeting and he couldn't imagine why.

Dave investigated and found something surprising and shocking. His bank was reporting him for not paying his entire mortgage payment-even though he was paying the amount the bank told him to pay.

Dave, of course, contacted his bank the moment he discovered the unfortunate state of his credit. He asked the "real human" at the bank what was the meaning of this? He was told, unbelievably, that since he was not paying the full amount of the *original* mortgage amount that they had no choice but to report him as late. By this time, about 18 months had ticked by, even though as I have mentioned, under H.A.M.P. guidelines Dave was supposed to have a firm answer-one way or the other-if he qualified for a mortgage modification in three months (*not* 18).

Dave asked, *"What can I do?"* The bank's reply: *"Pay what you owe us, or we will foreclosure on your home."* Dave asked, *"But what about the mortgage modification process?"* The "real human" said, *"It says here on my screen, that you did not qualify. We sent you a notice."* Apparently the bank was not only good about "losing" the paperwork Dave was sending, but they also "lost" the proper mailing address to send

Dave his mortgage modification decline notice *3 months ago.*

So where did all those mortgage payments go for those 18 months? Why was Dave reported as late? In case you missed this point, earlier in the book, it bears repeating: not one dime of the money Dave payed in those 18 months went to his mortgage. I repeat, in the eyes of the bank he was not paying his mortgage. So where did that money go? The bank used it to keep the property taxes and the insurance current. As mentioned earlier, during my interview on MSNBC (about 2 minutes into the video), I explain this. The odds are that after this H.A.M.P. odyssey, Dave would lose his house and the bank knew this.

Also, Dave had relied on the bank to give him an answer on the status of this loan modification. For all those months Dave assumed the bank was working away on the approval of his loan modification, so he continued to spend the "extra money" to improve his home and pay his bills. He had not anticipated a scenario such as this, so he never put that money aside while he waited to see if he qualified for H.A.M.P. He relied on the bank's promise to his detriment. (Remember *detrimental reliance?*).

According to H.A.M.P. guidelines-those set by our federal government, one aspect that is so simple is the 31% formula. If the bank employee had just taken a simple calculator, they would have seen that-before *any* paperwork was received (or not) that Dave was in a home he could not afford. Because of this, there was no amount close to 31% of Dave's pre-tax income that could have been lowered that much to pay off his mortgage. They could have put Dave in a 60 or 70 year mortgage, and, based on Dave's modest income and the buying price of Dave's home, mathematically it **never** *would have worked*. Remember, Dave is not an economist. He was relying on the bank, *the financial professionals*, to tell him this news. Instead, as you know, the bank strung Dave along for a year and a half.

In the MSNBC video with Dave, Bank of America's public relations spokesperson said that if Dave would just send the documents again (he had already sent the same documents 3 times) they could offer him a non-H.A.M.P. modification. The problem with this offer is, because of being in the H.A.M.P. "nightmare," Dave's credit was destroyed so he would never be able to qualify for *any* kind of loan.

Dave, now severely in the financial "hole," and now in retirement, had no money to hire an attorney. While I had helped clients battle loan scammers, Dave's case was one of the first that involved a large bank. Knowing what I knew about H.A.M.P. I was angry and ready to take it on. I just had to convince Dave who was understandably emotionally and financially beaten down.

Why Would the Bank Want My Home to Go into Foreclosure?

Before we continue on in this book, this is a question I feel is important to answer. It is not going to be an easy answer. If you were to search the answer to this question on the Internet, you will find various "solutions." Some will tell you, "Of course the bank does not want to foreclose!" They will tell you it's expensive for them to start foreclosure proceedings. That is true-it is expensive. When you read *my* answer you may feel as if you woke up in an alternate universe where nothing makes sense, so hang in there with me as I explain.

Let's go back to Dave. As I explained earlier, as Dave was paying his mortgage payments during the H.A.M.P. trial period, that money was going towards property taxes and insurance. Dave believed the money he was paying each month was going toward his mortgage payments-that belief is *incorrect*.

While Dave was in the H.A.M.P. trial period, the bank "identified" him as a homeowner who was a "risk" and could very possibly not afford his mortgage payments. When Dave was "identified," the bank's internal accounting system sent out an "alarm," of sorts. The alarm meant that when Dave paid his trial H.A.M.P. payments, the bank knew to put these payments aside in an escrow account to "protect" the home-the bank's asset *in anticipation* of a foreclosure.

The bank benefits monetarily the longer the H.A.M.P. trial period is. The longer the trial period, the more money the bank can collect from Dave who is at home waiting for an answer. By having Dave hold on as long as possible, the bank is storing away money that will protect *their* house. Dave wants to take the bank's claims of lost documents, etc. at face value and wants to believe the bank really did lose all those documents 3 times. However, the bank was using this as a delaying tactic to keep Dave hanging on *and paying.*

The money in the escrow account pays for property taxes and insurance on the home (fire, vandals, etc.). In anticipation of Dave not being able to pay his mortgage, the bank has an "alarm" system in place to protect the asset that will eventually go back to the bank.

There is a second "tier" to this "alarm" system. Behind the scenes, investors have purchased a type of "foreclosure insurance." In this case, this "foreclosure insurance" is payed out *to the bank* when Dave goes into foreclosure.

I am explaining this "two tiered alarm" system in the simplest terms. It is very complex. Investors, the bank's board of directors, and many other high level decision makers are involved in the purchase of this insurance to protect *their* assets.

As you can imagine it as a "win" (for lack of a better word) for the bank if Dave goes into foreclosure. The bank collects (1) all that money that Dave paid during the H.A.M.P trial as well as (2) proceeds from this "foreclosure insurance," (3) as well as money from the *new buyer* of Dave's home.

While it may seem that Dave is their client and in business we are taught to make the client happy, the true people that bank needs to make happy are their investors and board of directors. Dave's happiness is a lower priority to the bank. I'm sure it comes as no surprise to you that the bank is in business to make money-*for* it's investors, board, etc.

You may argue, but what about society? Isn't it bad business to let homes go into foreclosure, and let cities and towns decline? Rationally, do you believe the bank is in business to improve society? I repeat, the bank is in business to make money.

Another reason, Dave's home went into foreclosure is two things I encounter constantly: (1) unskilled banking employees who deal with Dave directly (and have little idea of the "big picture" of why Dave's H.A.M.P trial period is being delayed), and (2) a bank that is too big. The bank is too big and has too many unskilled employees to adequately process Dave's loan, locate Dave's paperwork, etc. Every month when Dave personally spoke to a "real human" at the bank, it was always a *different* "real human," talking to thousands of "Daves" a day. Since the bank is there to make money, it is very likely that the "real human" was not really paid all that well to personally care about Dave or where his paperwork was, or that his credit was being destroyed.

Whether Dave is happy or not, the employee still receives his or her $6-10 an hour. This is common of many large companies. The people with the finance degrees and life experience in the banking field are not the ones who are dealing with Dave directly. Those with the experience are managing hoards of untrained "real humans" in your community and overseas.

A Dose of Reality About the Legal World

As I mentioned briefly at the beginning of this book, my theory of arguing your case can be used in a higher court. This section is for those of you still "on the fence" about small claims. You may look at your state's low small claims limits and wonder if this is a fight worth pursuing. If that is the case, please read on.

Perhaps you've seen those news stories-the ones where the client defiantly stands beside their attorney who proudly declares, *"We are sending a message to the bank. We are not giving up the fight, especially when it is a fight for justice! We are going to take on the bank!"*

I proudly work with attorneys. I "rub elbows with them" and attend many Bar Association functions. One thing I can assure you is that very few attorneys work for free. Many lay people seem to think that attorneys are serving a "higher calling" and will defend their honor (and their case) forever in an effort to "fight for justice" and "send a message." This thinking is just not based in reality. There *are* many attorneys who would love to spend their life bettering our world, but the fact is they have to pay their bills just like you. In the vast majority of cases, attorneys are not in business to provide free services.

I hear many homeowners say they cannot get a lawyer to take their case. Some lawyers may take your case *at first,* but as your money runs out (and it runs out fast), your lawyer will likely avoid your phone calls.

People that view the world idealistically view the legal field the way they view the health care field. *Who wouldn't want to live in an ideal world?* Regardless of how you feel about the issue politically, in an ideal world, it would be wonderful if we all had access to free health care and free legal advice and free *whatever else we needed.* The problem is, this is *not* an ideal world, and health care, like legal advice is expensive. I think we can also agree that when we are in need of both, we are usually in a state of desperation.

Having worked in this field for nearly 20 years, it is not enough for you to go in to court thinking that you can tell your very emotional story and the judge will grant you anything you desire. The hard-to-swallow reality is that just because what happened to you is morally and ethically wrong, it may not be *illegal.* On the other hand, if it *is* illegal, the attorney that you hire will probably hire several very pricey experts to prove that theory-and you will have to pay the bill.

More reality: If you do hire an attorney, they too will have to be compensated, again for several thousands of dollars, before the attorney even begins to look at one contract between you and your lender. It has been my experience that attorneys "eat" through that initial retainer at a rapid pace because not only are they paying themselves, they are searching behind the scenes to hire experts to prove your case. Hollywood would have you believe that the attorney just has to say something emotional and compelling and you claim victory-*it is just not that simple.*

Speaking of experts, you were no doubt emotionally scarred from this entire experience. While proving a case in court you will have to hire an additional expert to testify just how emotionally distraught you were. You may have to hire a court approved psychiatrist to go through your medical records, then testify what you have been through. If your health has been affected, it is the same process-you will have to hire a physician expert to first thoroughly go through your medical records and then convince the jury how physically and/or emotionally devastated you were. It is not nearly as simple as you telling the jury how hurt you were by the bank. Hollywood works that way-*real world courts don't.*

The point I am trying to make, and ask you to consider, is the expense of the process of fighting back in higher courts. If you are reading this book, you are very likely financially devastated. Another issue I would like you to consider is time. You have probably wasted so much time and energy dealing with this topic. The real world court system is not know for their "speediness." You experienced delay tactics first hand in your mortgage modification process. You can only imagine the delaying tactics deployed when a court battle is involved.

In my final plea, I would like to share something with you personally about a family member of mine. I have their permission to share this.

I have a family member who was severely hurt at work. He needed a lot of medical treatment and unfortunately, was on the receiving end of medical malpractice that left him permanently disabled. It, in itself, is a very long story.

He found an attorney who took his case and the discovery phase-or the building of the case phase-was underway. The preparation from the time he was injured until we all sat in front of a jury was 10 years.

During those 10 years he was no longer able to work because he was so severely injured-so that was 10 years without his income. He also was followed and photographed to try and "catch" him acting like a well person. The phenomenon of looking over his shoulder for 10 years did a lot to his psyche. He was interviewed countless times by court approved experts. Everything he said was scrutinized and turned inside out. For 10 years he went back and forth with lawyers who debated his story even though it was physically apparent how hurt he was. The other side tried to "poke holes" in everything he said, and everything he did. I imagine the other side knew how hurt he was but it was their job to wear him down on behalf of *their* client-the doctor who's mistake was the cause of his injury.

Going before a jury is not a common experience in civil matters (as opposed to criminal matters). In higher courts, approximately 2% of cases actually are presented to a jury. The other 98% are settled. This does not mean that the other 98% are bad cases or even weak cases. They are settled for many reasons. People get worn down, they need some money to move forward with their lives, the legal costs start to outweigh the final reward-the reasons are many.

Finally, after a decade of debates, scrutiny, and being watched, the jury heard his case-it took about 1 month. It was an emotional month as his life hung in the balance. The jury sat stone faced so we were never aware how, or if, they were understanding all the complex medical information. It was emotional to sit across the room from the doctors who had hurt him so badly-and permanently. It was emotional to hear statements that were totally fabricated to make his case appear weaker. By the time the jury heard everything, the family was a wreck. A lot of tears were shed on the stand and at his home in the evening. It was painful for him to relive all that he had been through. He said it truly was like going through the ordeal all over again as every detail had to be unearthed and scrutinized and debated. Over 15 experts were paraded before the jury and over $100,000 was spent to make the case.

After about the long trial, the jury made their decision in a little over an hour. Ten years of experiences that changed his life forever and they were able to decide his fate in one hour? We were sure he had lost.

The fact is *he won.* To many of us, the jury awarded what would be considered a lifetime of money. We celebrated for a few hours but when we returned to his home reality set in as the family "digested" the decade of events.

Had he been working all those years, he would have made many times that amount. He would have had his health and the ability to continue a career that he deeply loved and sacrificed for, working nights, weekends, and holidays to pay the schooling for.

When we realized the legal "hell" he had lived through for a decade, we slowly began to realize how life would have been easier and more enjoyable if he did not have to spend 10 years turning over "every rock" and relive every painful memory. He would have not had to look over his shoulder. He would have been able to speak freely with his doctor and not fear that anything he said would be perceived by the chart's reader as "not really hurt that bad." It was a victory for him, but a hollow one, because he was *still* permanently injured, the doctors who caused the injury got to continue their careers, and the money-while it made a difference initially-never completely compensated him for all he had experienced.

Only you will ever understand the price you have paid in going through your H.A.M.P. nightmare. You may have suffered a divorce, a stroke, or something else that will have a life long impact. What many of my clients find, after they really, really think about it is, even if they were handed a large pile of money, they still wish they did not have to go through the ordeal. I am not telling you about my family member's personal experience to talk you out of pursuing legal action-quite the opposite. While money is extremely important-and who knows that more when they don't have any, there are other things that you should consider if you were to sue your bank in a higher court.

So what choices does that leave you with? The title of this book, Sue Your Bank-For *Little or No Money, Make Sense of Your*

H.A.M.P. Nightmare, & Take Back Your Life!-is about taking charge of your situation without going broke or spending years fighting.

If you followed Dave's story, you may know that Dave fought his bank in small claims court. You may have even considered it yourself until you found out how little compensation you would receive if you were to win your case. You may have even watched an episode of Judge Judy and wondered how you would ever fight something as complicated as arguing with your bank is such a venue.

Going to small claims court can give you a resolution to the issues with the bank in a few months and cost very little. I know the prospect can sound daunting, but I have done this multiple times. I can show you what to say, you can possibly get yourself a settlement, prove fraud, restore your credit, and truly move forward with your life.

Still not entirely convinced? Let me share with you a conversation I have with many who call me to weigh their options. Understandably, many are outraged at the mention of small claims court. They see it as "settling" when their life is being turned "upside down." Consider this conversation with Joe from California who's small claims court limits are $10,000. (California's small claims limits were lifted on 1/2012 from $7,500 to $10,000):

Client: "Hi Mr. Sims. I saw your video and wanted to explore my options. I love that Dave fought back and won, but for all I've been through-all that my family has been through-I just can't fight for $10,000!"

Sims: "Thanks for your call Joe. I completely understand how you feel and many others feel the same way. I can offer you these options: (1) Hire an attorney...."

Client: "I can't afford an attorney."

Sims: "...or, (2) go to small claims court. Here is what happens with many of my clients when they choose this option: For many, just the act of filing the suit made the bank pay attention. A bank rep showed up to court, they, along with the homeowner, met with a court mediator. The two came to an agreement (for some that was the offer of another loan mod [if they were able to work with their credit score], for others, a settlement). Because they are in court, their agreement is backed by an order from the judge forcing the bank to follow through-all done in small claims court. For many homeowners, more important than a settlement or loan modification was the judge ordering the bank to restore the homeowner's credit. As you know with a wrecked credit score you are almost held hostage and cannot move forward with your life- you cannot get a job, an apartment, car, etc. I wrote a book called "Sue Your Bank" that explains these options. Want more money out of your lawsuit? You will have to go to a higher court, hire a lawyer or represent yourself and possibly spend years fighting. Regardless of the level of court, the book shows you the theories I argue that are acceptable in any court. The book is written in a very easy to understand way. You don't have to have a law degree to understand it. I wish I could offer you more options, Joe, but this is an option that can work and it is affordable. Sadly, I don't see any of the experts in the media offering other, affordable options."

Client: "I guess I've never considered this option before and the reality of my situation. Thanks Mr. Sims. You've given me a lot to think about."

Many of the people that contact me looking for options take several months to think about it. It is not an easy decision when you have been through so much.

****

For those of you who have the finances and time to pursue a lawsuit in a higher court, hire a lawyer or even represent yourself, these theories can work in a higher court. Whatever you decide, I hope you will read on how this is possible.

For those of you who are wondering if you can even afford going to small claims court, I will share some options as well.

To help you decide, this next section is about Dave and what he went through in his own small claims battle. I believe you will see that if Dave could do it then *you can too!*

A Peek Inside Dave's Battle

When I formed CLCREE in 2009[11] H.A.M.P. was just being announced. Thousands of so-called "experts" and "specialists" were already lining up to "help" homeowners in very creative ways.

Banks apparently were also "helping" in creative ways. By the time the bank was done with Dave, he had little money left to hire an attorney. There were plenty of organizations and law firms out there offering their help. The majority wanted several thousand dollars (to start). Dave contacted me. I was behind the scenes working in this field (remember the anesthesiologist scenario). I was teaching judges and attorneys about how to take on mortgage scammers and banks. In working within the nonprofit, I knew from experience that homeowners were in need of help but did not have the funds to wage a large legal battle. We had many successes-if the scammers had not "skipped town," but fighting a bank was new. This was definitely uncharted territory.

Though each state varies in their small claims programs, in California, attorneys are

---

[11] The name has been changed to "Courtroom Advocates."

not permitted. You can however bring an expert. For example, if you are arguing about a car, you can bring a mechanic to testify. Dave brought me.

So Dave and I went to court. The dialog below is an actual transcript of what happened. I have included it because I want you to see that it is not as difficult as it may have played out in your mind. You will see that Dave did not have to make a long speech or memorize and argue complicated legal concepts. I included this to take the fear out of the unknown. Having said that, each judge runs his courtroom differently. If the plan in this book sounds like something you would like to explore, I urge you to attend your local small claims court at least twice to see how the judge conducts things. Despite what you will read in small claims books, in each individual courtroom the judge is in charge and each courtroom is run differently.

Since this was my first case fighting a big bank (in small claims court, that is), I learned a few things. After Dave's hearing I figured I could also teach my clients to ask for more than just money in their "damages" by the bank. With clients *after* Dave, I taught them to ask to have their credit restored. Having good-or even fair credit-is a fact of life in America and almost like a "golden ticket." It allows you buy necessities of our lives, such as a car and even get a decent apartment. It may even matter if you are hired at a particular job. It is a valuable thing and you should stay vigilant on it. If you were, or are in H.A.M.P., your credit was very likely destroyed. Asking for the judge to restore your credit-which is something he has the power to do-*is a very important reason why you should fight back.* Yes, if you win, you will win *some* money, but it is your credit score restored that will truly allow you to move forward with your life. This reason alone may be worth the fight-even in those states who unfortunately only offer as little as $2,500 in their small claims court limits.

Alan R. Sims

Court Transcript of Dave's Battle

I have included the actual transcript so you can read what takes place when you go to small claims. Don't let small claims fool you. The only difference between small claims and other courts is the cost, the time spent and the reward amount. As you read the transcript you will see how the ability to tell your story is the same. The transcript offers a "window" into what it is like to tell your story before a judge. There was also a mediation between Bank of America's representative and Dave. I was not allowed to be present for this exchange but Dave reported it "went nowhere." We will talk about mediations later in this book.

Not all states offer a small claims courtroom transcript. Some do not keep a record of the testimony. In this court, the testimony was taped, and I was allowed access to a copy of the tape. There was no court reporter. This is a transcript of what was on the tape:

Graham v. Bank of America

Judge John Pacheco

Plaintiff: David Graham

Expert for the Plaintiff: Alan R. Sims of The Center for Litigation & Consumer Real Estate Education (now Courtroom Advocates).

Defendant: Anthony Lopez, Bank of America

****

Judge: Graham vs. Bank of America. Good Afternoon.

Plaintiff: Good afternoon, your honor.

Defendant Bank: Good afternoon, your honor.

Judge: Good afternoon. Wait a minute. This is David Graham...(as he shuffles court documents).

Plaintiff: That's correct.

Judge: ...vs. Bank of America?

Defendant Bank: Yes sir.

Judge: And your name sir (directed to Defendant)?

Defendant Bank: Anthony Lopez, your honor.

Judge: Anthony Lopez (makes a note). What is your position with Bank of America?

Defendant Bank: I'm a mortgage servicer. A mortgage service specialist with outreach group.

Judge: (making a note). Mortgage servicer specialist?

Defendant Bank: Yes sir.

Judge: Does specialist mean that you have some specialty?

Defendant Bank: Yes your honor.

Judge: What do you specialize in?

Defendant Bank: Umm. Non-contractual modifications.

Judge: What does "non-contractual" mean?

Defendant Bank: Modifications that have to do with borrowers outside of non-contractual agencies.

Judge: (makes a note) Borrowers outside of non- contractual agencies?

Defendant Bank: Yes, your honor.

Judge: (still making a note). Non-contractual agencies. All right. Mr. Graham is bringing a claim against...so you're here on behalf of Bank of America?

Defendant Bank: Bank of America, your honor.

Judge (making a note). OK. But Mr. Graham is bringing a claim for $7,500,* claiming that this was a fraudulent home loan modification. Is that correct?

Since this case, California has raised their small claims court limits to $10,000.

Plaintiff: That's correct your honor.

Judge: All right. You don't have any exhibits? (Directing question to bank representative).

Defendant Bank: All exhibits are on a secured lap top that belongs to the company. I was unable to print it out. Critical documents.

Judge: But did you show your documents to the other side even though they were digital or electronic?

Defendant Bank: I did not, your honor.

Judge: You do not or you did not?

Defendant Bank: I did not show them.

Judge: OK.

Defendant Bank: I wasn't aware that we could just display digital documentation.

Judge: Well, if you wanted to argue certain things certainly may need a new computer.

Defendant Bank: Mine's in there.

Judge: So did you get some documents from them?

Defendant Bank: Uh, they did share documents with me.

Judge: All right. So the allegation is a fraudulent home loan. Is that correct?

Plaintiff: That's correct.

Judge: Mr. Graham, how is it that you came to the belief that it was a fraudulent home loan?

Plaintiff: Your honor, I feel that I was taken unfair advantage of by the defendants when they approached me with the purpose of involving me in a, uh, home loan modification under the H.A.M.P. program. Under the guidelines of that program my monthly mortgage would not have been able to exceed 31% of my monthly gross income. Um...

Judge: um hum

Plaintiff:..which it certainly did.

Judge: By how much more? Do you have any idea?

Plaintiff: Well, I have a chart here that states what I would have had to have made monthly to qualify myself for it...for the mortgage.

Judge: Have you shown that document to the Defendant?

Plaintiff: Yes.

Judge: Let me see that. (Bailiff takes document from Plaintiff and hands it to the judge). So you would have had to make...how much money were you making per month?

Plaintiff: Uh, I am making approximately $26,000 a year so it would have been about $2,200 a month.

Judge: OK. And so basically you would have **had to make a salary almost three times more.** Right?

Plaintiff: That's correct.

Judge: OK. And this mortgage calculator[12] (referring to exhibit) you put this together? You ran this program...this calculator is just a standard program. Right? Ok. So you didn't like fix the numbers or anything like that?

Plaintiff: (laughs) No, your honor.

Judge: So the loan amount was $200,000?

Plaintiff: The loan amount that was on the home at the time was about $200,000.

Judge: OK. All right. So I've got the first document. We'll mark that as exhibit 1 (directing the court clerk). And then what happened? So they, uh, did they tell you you'd qualify? What did they tell you?

Plaintiff: They told me that because of the type of loan that I had that, uh, I was eligible to apply for this mortgage modification and

---

[12] *In May 2011, H.A.M.P. unveiled a calculator.[12] Perhaps since the bank was doing "such a great job" letting you know if you qualified, the federal government thought why not help the homeowner see if they qualify? Just my opinion. (Dave's trial took place in January 2011 and I had a calculator sheet on my website available for my clients). The chart the judge is speaking of is in the appendices of this book. It is based on the 31% H.A.M.P. rule we discussed earlier in this book. You may bring a copy to court to show the judge.*

that it would take approximately 90 days to get an answer whether I'd get it or not. That I would qualify.

Judge: OK. And did they have this information that you put on exhibit 1 already when they told you you were eligible to apply?

Plaintiff: No, your honor.

Judge: Well, in order for them to tell you that you were eligible to apply did they have some income and expense information from you? Did you fill out an income...

Plaintiff: I did send them some information of my income. Yes.

Judge:...verification? So they knew that, uh, what your income was?

Plaintiff: That's correct, your honor.

Judge: OK. And still, based on the information that you sent them, um, they told you that you were eligible to apply?

Plaintiff: That's correct.

Judge: All right. And is it your belief that now, in hindsight, that you were *not* eligible to apply?

Plaintiff: Not by the guidelines that were provided by the H.A.M.P. program.

Judge: So what happened?

Plaintiff: Uh, well, we proceeded to agree upon an, um, a reduced monthly mortgage amount. They reduced my mortgage by $400.00 a month during this trial period which was supposed to be about 90 days, um, during which they requested more information which had been sent already. They said they did not, um, have the information.

Judge: About how many times did you have to send the same exact information that you had sent to them?

Plaintiff: I believe I sent information to them 3 different times.

Judge: Three different times?

Plaintiff: (acknowledges yes)

Judge: And you sent it the first time? The second time they said they misplaced it? They lost it?

Plaintiff: They said there was some incomplete information that they would need. Some further information.

Judge: OK. Was it...when you sent the further information was it the exact same information you had sent before?

Plaintiff: Uh, it would have been current pay stubs and, uh, tax return information and that.

Judge: OK. So then what happened?

Plaintiff: Uh, the uh...I continued to make the forbearance payments on a monthly basis. Uh, I chose to do it through the telephone so that I would be in touch with them on a monthly basis. Every month I had asked the representative that I talked to, which was a different one each time, uh, what the progress was, and I was told that my account was still under review and that I should continue to make forbearance payments. This went on for about 18 months. Uh, during that 18 month period I received notices from some other creditors stating that they were reducing my credit amount due to some reported, uh, late mortgage payments. And when I contacted, I believe it was BAC (Bank of America Credit) Loan Servicing. They had explained to me that because there was a difference between what I was paying and what I was contracted to pay under my mortgage and that they had to report that difference as late mortgage payments.

Judge: So it affected your credit?

Plaintiff: It affected my credit drastically. I was not behind my mortgage payments when I go into this agreement with Bank of America and BAC.

Judge: OK. So they said you were eligible to apply. They reduced your mortgage payments by $400.00 a month. Which you did. Every time you went to make a payment you would call telephonically to check on the status. And you went through different numbers of agents?

Plaintiff: That's correct.

Judge: And then out, *wah-lah*, your credit has been damaged because you quote-unquote made your, you were late on your mortgage payments?

Plaintiff: Correct.

Judge: OK. Did they tell you that when they said you were eligible to apply and that you could reduce your mortgage...did they tell you that, uh, by you paying a lesser amount that this could affect your credit?

Plaintiff: No your honor.

Judge: Did you receive any written documentation that would substantiate, or show, in the written documentation that, uh, this could affect your credit?

Plaintiff: No

Judge: OK. So then you found out that you had been reported to a credit agency-then what happened?

Plaintiff: Uh, approximately 18 months after I engaged in this, uh, which would have been about September of this year (2010), um, I received a notice from the Bank of America stating I would have to pay them somewhere in the neighborhood of $7,000 within about 30 day period to make my mortgage current or they would proceed with foreclosure process on my home.

Judge: OK. So they tell you that you're eligible to apply. They reduce your mortgage by $400.00. You conform with all their requirements by paying your mortgage every month. $400 less, like they told you. And every month you call them for 18 months and then you find out that they have, or someone reported you to a credit agency. And they tell you now, "Hey, you want to make your mortgage current, you have to pay $7,000.00?

Plaintiff: That's correct, your honor.

Judge: Doesn't seem fair.

Plaintiff: No. It certainly doesn't.

Judge: Did you, do you believe were you were induced, fraudulently induced into this so that way you would fail on your mortgage?

Plaintiff: I can't say what the reason would have been. I don't see why somebody would do that. But, uh, we were certainly, uh, lead to believe we were going to qualify for this in the long term. And, um, all the while of course, was destroying my credit and the end result is that they were planing on taking my home from me.

Judge: Have you received a notice of foreclosure?

Plaintiff: I have received notice of foreclosure. Yes.

Judge: By who?

Plaintiff: By Bank of America.

Judge: The same bank that asked you, and told you, that you were eligible to apply?

Plaintiff: That's correct.

Judge: Was there anything that you did, or did not do, that made you ineligible?

Plaintiff: Not that I'm aware of, your honor.

Judge: Did anything change from the time they told you you were eligible to apply until the time they said you had to come up with $7,000.00 and they were going to foreclosure on your house? Did your income change? Did you stop paying?

Plaintiff: I, uh, I had retired within that period of time which I had mentioned to them. I told them when I initially got into this that my income had been reduced and that it was going to be reduced further when I retired.

Judge: Did you give them the documentation as to how much it was going to be reduced by?

Plaintiff: At the time, I did not have exact numbers on that, your honor.

Judge: OK. All right. So how long had you lived in your house?

Plaintiff: Uh, I have been there since 2002.

Judge: Wow, so your coming up...so you're probably past eight years now?

Plaintiff: That's correct.

Judge: And, you're going to lose your house?

Plaintiff: Yes sir.

Judge: OK. So you're bringing a claim...are there any documents you'd like to introduce?

Plaintiff: Uh, I do have a few documents referring to the H.A.M.P. program here. Number one, the, uh, the document that, uh, stipulates the 31% debt-to-income ratio. *And I have a document here that does indicate that if a borrower is current when they engage into this agreement that they cannot be reported as late.*

Judge: They cannot be reported as late?

Plaintiff: Yes. That's correct. (Plaintiff hands document to bailiff who hands them to judge).

Judge: Hmmm. Any other documents...well have you shown these documents to the defendant?

Plaintiff: Yes.

Judge: OK. And you have...

Plaintiff: I do have with me, your honor, my professional witness, Mr. Alan Sims here today to testify on my behalf also.

Judge: What would Mr. Sims, if he were called to testify to?

Plaintiff: I believe he would testify, uh, that this, uh, is a regular practice with some of the banks involved in the H.A.M.P. program today, and that, uh, more people than just myself are being taken advantage of, uh, in this way.

Judge: OK. Well I'm not really concerned with about the other people. This is your case, so as it pertains to your case, is your expert that you have today, that he would testify, that you were damaged? OK. All right, call your witness.

Plaintiff's Expert (herein referred to as "Expert"): Good Afternoon, your honor.

Judge: Your name sir?

Expert: My name is Alan Sims (spells name).

Judge: Mr. Sims. Uh, I know you. [13]

---

[13] *The judge knew me from the County Bar Association functions I attend and I had been in his court before on other matters.*

Expert: Yes sir.

Judge: You have a different haircut?

Expert: About 68 pounds lighter.

Judge: And you're a little bit lighter. Didn't recognize you at first. You've been here before, haven't you sir?

Expert: Yes sir, we've been here a number of times with loan modification scammers over the last two years. My organization, The Center for Litigation & Consumer Real Estate Education. We act as a consumer advocacy group, as well as, we assist the public in pursuing loan modification, mortgage fraud, or anything real estate related.

Judge: Did you assist Mr. Graham on his loan modification?

Expert: No sir. I assisted Mr. Graham, uh, on analyzing what happened to him and whether or not there was a potential here for Bank of America to make any type of fraudulent act against Mr. Graham.

Judge: What makes you an expert in this regard?

Expert: Uh, I teach mortgage fraud, the elements of it, as well as I study the H.A.M.P. program in the way that the banks administer this program and not administer this program in mismanage this program.

Judge: About how many H.A.M.P. (spells it) programs type loans have you worked on?

Expert: I have worked inquiries, your honor, I get them nationwide. We're looking at about 680 at this stage.

Judge: And you say you also teach it. How long have you been teaching?

Expert: I've been teaching mortgage fraud for attorneys for over 4 years. It's approved by the State Bar of California.

Judge: Approximately how many classes have you conducted?

Expert: In the last 4 years I have at least conducted a dozen classes. The last class I gave on ethics was in October this year with the High Desert Bar.

Judge: OK. So have you looked at any documents involving Mr. David Graham?

Expert: Uh, yes sir, I have.

Judge: What documents did you look at?

Expert: Uh, when he came to my office, he showed me the payments that he was making to the mortgage company. I also interviewed Mr. Graham the same way you did today, sir. Basically, there was a disconnect with what he was telling me, what he was paying for the mortgage, because he was current on his payments. Prior to going and being solicited by Bank of America. He wasn't late. And it was just a mass mailing he received. He then he called up Bank of America, at least what he was telling me about how his income was going to be reduced to $26,400.00 and Bank of America wanted to go ahead and reduce his mortgage each month by $400.00. That would help him out with his retirement. And in turn, I was questioning Mr. Graham saying well how can you take care of a $200,000.00 mortgage making less money? This was never addressed to him by B of A during this period of time. All his solicitations were done, and his agreements were done, on the phone. He has no written contract that Bank of America sent him for any of this modification. There is nothing that he was ever produced except for what he was given as his loan payment. Now...

Judge: Did you not, uh, in order to be eligible to apply, didn't you have to fill out some documents?

Plaintiff: There were no documents sent to me.

Judge: And you, Mr. Graham, it's your testimony that you called Bank of America every month?

Plaintiff: That's correct.

Judge: To make your payment?

Plaintiff: That's correct.

Judge: And you inquired at that time to check on your eligibility?

Plaintiff: That's correct, your honor.

Judge: And at any time when you did that for the eighteen months did they ever tell you, "You don't apply. You need to sign this document," or anything like that?

Plaintiff: No.

Judge: No? OK. Anything else?

Expert: Yes, your honor. This is affecting close to about 500,000 people in the United States. Uh..

Judge: Again, I'm not worried about the 500,000. I'm worried about this person. 'Cause this is...we're not a 500,000 class action case here.

Expert: I understand that. This is not class action. But this is similar in nature what is happening to everyone. They claim they lose paper work. Over the phone they give promises. Mr. Graham doesn't want to lose his home. He wanted to go stop the foreclosure any way he can. Mr. Graham made these trial modified payments, and then after supposedly 90 days, that's the government program that they have to have a "yeah," or "nay," decision. You can't keep taking money without a net result. They can extend them out in 2 years. 21 months, is average to get a yes or no answer back from Bank of America. And at the end there they say, "I'm sorry, you're not qualified."

Judge: So he went for eighteen months, 90 days plus eighteen months and he got a "nay?"

Expert: Yes, sir.

Judge: Which is their right. Correct?

Expert: I'm sorry?

Judge: They have a right to say, "No. You don't qualify."

Expert: Yes, but they're supposed to do it in 90 days sir.

Judge: Hmm. OK. All right. Anything else?

Expert: No sir.

Judge: (directed to Defendant Bank). Do you have any questions, Mr. Lopez, that you'd like to ask either Mr. Graham or Mr. Sims?

Defendant Bank: Yes, your honor, um, you did not receive any modification due to the bank, not M.H.A. modification,[14] but a bank modification shortly after, um, we believe, we did, I have proof, but once again it's in my computer, so I was not advised that I could I would say present digital documentation that we did send a decline letter for the M.H.A. solicitation.

Plaintiff: I did not...

Defendant Bank: Just shortly after, you did not receive any type of bank modification as far as manually done by the bank?

---

[14] *The bank representative is referring to Making Home Affordable (M.H.A.) which is the organization that oversees H.A.M.P.*

Plaintiff: I did not receive any notification as far as that's concerned.

Defendant Bank: As far as to my knowledge that's what we had sent.

Judge: Any other questions you'd like to ask either the expert or Mr. Graham?

Defendant Bank: No, your honor.

Judge: OK. Is there anything that you'd like to argue (directed to the defendant)?

Defendant Bank: In this case, due to the fact that it was M.H.A. modification, um, after a borrower is done with trial payments, they are subject to underwriting review. Uh, if anything has changed financially, or anything is missing, as far as documents, um, it would therefore, we would reach out to the borrower, and contact, which I did not see in our note system, which is not printable.

Judge: OK. So it's YOU that calls the borrower? It's not them having to call you just to check on status?

Defendant Bank: During...

Judge: It's you that calls and gets the information?

Defendant Bank: Correct, your honor.

Judge: How many times did you call him?

Defendant Bank: Well, it wasn't me personally.

Judge: Well, I know. How many times did your, as a representative, how many times did you?

Plaintiff: As a representative we are to make three contact attempts.

Judge: OK. What days did you make those attempts?

Plaintiff: I don't have them in front of me, your honor.

Judge: OK. Who made the attempts?

Plaintiff: Um, they would be negotiators within the modification department.

Judge: OK.

Defendant Bank: Not one solitary person.

Judge: OK. So your custom and practice is that there is supposed to make three attempts. You don't have the documentation that it was made, but that's your custom and practice?

Defendant Bank: Yes, your honor.

Judge: And you don't know the names of the people that made those attempts?

Defendant Bank: No, your honor.

Judge: Although you have digital documentation, you didn't keep documentation of when you made a phone call?

Plaintiff: I do have the digital documentation. It's in a note system that we do, that we do use.

Judge: Uh huh

Defendant Bank: That is basically not printable. It's in a note system that we do to archive our conversations.

Judge: But you refresh your own recollection by looking at those digital notes and you can tell me the exact dates when those calls were made. The time it was made. And who made them. Correct?

Defendant Bank: Correct? Would you mind if I...

Judge: No. Go ahead.

Defendant Bank: (searching through computer)

Judge: I mean they're basically saying that you didn't ever call them and they called you?

Defendant Bank: Right.

Judge: (jokingly) I might have to keep that as an exhibit (meaning computer).

Defendant Bank: (laughs. Computer makes noise.)

Judge: That didn't sound good.

Defendant Bank: Yeah. (still searching through computer).

Judge: All right. When did you...while he's looking through that information, when did you, when were you advised that you were eligible to apply?

Plaintiff: That would have been on or about March, 2009; right about the time that the government instituted the H.A.M.P. program.

Judge: And, was it you that contacted, uh, Bank of America after you received something in the mail?

Plaintiff: Yes.

Judge: So they sent you something in the mail?

Plaintiff: Yes.

Judge: Do you have that document?

Plaintiff: I do not. (inaudible)

Judge: But it was right around March 2009?

Plaintiff: That's correct.

Judge: And so you called them. Did they make you forward some information to them?

Plaintiff: Yes. At that time they requested my financial information and my tax return information to be sent to them.

Judge: Did you in fact do that?

Plaintiff: Yes I did.

Judge: Do you remember if that was done it March or April?

Plaintiff: Uh, it would have been...

Judge: Or sometime after that?

Plaintiff: Right. Right within that time period. March or April.

Judge: OK. (Directed to Defendant Bank). So that way you can look on your log how many times. What dates did you make those calls?

Defendant Bank: Uh, your honor, there was contact attempts made on the 28th, that would be the 26th of April, which was the second attempt. Following the 23rd, as well as there was an attempt which showed documented as the third attempt to contact on the 27th of April. This would be 2010.

Judge: All right. And on those three attempts was there actual contact made?

Defendant Bank: No, um, as far as it is noted, they were assisting the underwriting process and they were trying to contact the homeowner for additional documents.

Judge: All right. So you have proof that three attempts were made?

Defendant Bank: Yes, your honor.

Judge: And, um do you have the names of the people that made those attempts?

Defendant Bank: They are logged in the system as actual company ID. NBK numbers is what we actually use. They are not identified by the actual name, just the NKB number.

Judge: Does it have an actual number that was called?

Defendant Bank: Yes it does, your honor. The number that was contacted was 909-XXX-XXXX.

Judge: Mr. Graham, is that your phone number?

Plaintiff: No it's not, your honor.

Judge: Have you ever had that number?

Plaintiff: No, your honor.

Judge: XXX-XXXX?

Plaintiff: No.

Judge: You have any idea where they got that phone call from? Or that phone number?

Plaintiff: No. (inaudible).

Judge: Did you give that to them?

Plaintiff: No I didn't.

Judge: Hmm.

Defendant Bank: Your honor, it is also possibility that there is a co-borrower on the loan by the name of Jane Graham.[15] Which she does have authorization to update phone numbers with collection associates when they do call in.

Judge: Um hum.

Defendant Bank: That's when we would update our contact information and erase any numbers that were on previously.

Judge: (directed to Plaintiff). Do you know who Jane Graham is?

Plaintiff: Yes, your honor.

Judge: Who's that?

Plaintiff: That's my ex-wife.

Judge: All right. And to your knowledge, has that ever been her number?

Plaintiff: No.

Judge: That's never been her number?

Plaintiff: No.

Judge: You've never called her at that number?

---

15 *Name changed to protect identity.*

Plaintiff: No.

Judge: Hmm. Do you have any other numbers on there? (directed to Defendant).

Defendant Bank: That's the only number I have, your honor.

Judge: OK. So all three numbers, all three attempts on the 23rd of April, the 26th of April, and the 27th of April-all three attempts were to this number?

Defendant Bank: Correct, your honor.

Judge: All right. Did they leave a note on there that they left messages?

Plaintiff: Yes, your honor. Also a number was left on the line; on that phone line that we did contact with a fax number to submit the documents that were missing in the M.H.A. process.

Judge: OK.

Defendant Bank: With a request to have those documents obtained in 72 hours.

Judge: 72 hours?

Defendant Bank: Yes, your honor.

Judge: Any other contacts that you have on that log of yours showing that you made over these 21 months?

Defendant Bank: Yes, uh, I do show that as far as the borrower was solicited again going back to the borrower was solicited with a manual modification, uh, due to the fact that the borrower does have a Fannie Mae loan. We did offer a Fannie Mae loan modification. I do have documents showing that as far as a modification being sent out.

Judge: OK. Just like he said, ineligible to apply?

Defendant Bank: Correct. M.H.A. is made on eligibility to apply. It does not mean that you are granted the modification due to the fact that it to go through an underwriting process after the trial period is over.

Judge: Does it, uh, did you hear what the expert and what Mr. Graham said? It was their understanding that you had to say yeah or nay within 90 days?

Defendant Bank: Yes, your honor.

Judge: OK. Do you have any proof that you said "yeah" or "nay" within 90 days?

Defendant Bank: I do have a decline letter for the M.H.A. program that was sent on May 21st, 2010 to the address of 2XX East XXXX Boulevard, Big Bear City, California, 92314.

Judge: OK. And that was sent on the 21st of May? So that would have been within the 90 days. Right?

Defendant Bank: Yes, your honor.

Judge: Hmm.

Defendant Bank: The modification also shortly followed. We did offer a solicited modification which did state on the letter that he has been approved for a manual modification which was sent on May 28th - just 7 days after the decline letter was sent on behalf of M.H.A.

Judge: So a manual modification. What is a manual modification?

Defendant Bank: A bank modification done by the bank. As they are going through the M.H.A./H.A.M.P. program.

Judge: OK. Mr. Graham, do you know; is that your address, 2XX East XXXX Boulevard?

Plaintiff: That's the address, yes.

Judge: OK. Did you ever receive that decline letter on the 21st of May?

Plaintiff: No, your honor. I did not. We, uh...

Judge: Did you ever receive a manual eligibility letter on the 28th of May?

Plaintiff: No sir. We do not receive mail at that address. It would have gone to a post office box, which I made clear to the bank all along.

Judge: So if someone; if I get an envelope and I write 2XX East XXXX Boulevard, what was it, Big Bear City?

Plaintiff: Big Bear City.

Judge: Big Bear City, and I put it in the mail is it going to get delivered to you?

Plaintiff: No sir. It would come back to you.

Judge: Uh oh. Because it's P.O. boxes only.

Plaintiff: That's correct.

Judge: Hmm. And did it come back to you (directed to Defendant Bank)?

Defendant Bank: As far as, it wouldn't come back to the department that sends them out, so any mail, that's a different line of business that I would not be able to, you know, explain what happened if mail came back.

Judge: Um hum. Well, I do unlawful detainers in the morning at 7:45, so I've been here all morning, and all day, but I do know that these lawyers they try to, uh, say that they sent it by mail to that address up in Big Bear and I've had the post master general person saying there is absolutely no way that the mail is delivered to people up in the mountains. It has to go to a P.O. box, and so I do know, I do have some facts, some knowledge that this happens like that. Were you aware of that (directed to Defendant Bank)?

Defendant Bank: I was not aware of that, your honor.

Judge: So, hmm.

Defendant Bank: As far as my system showed, it does show, property address and mailing address being the same. Once again, that can be changed by any borrower on the file.

Judge: Yeah, yeah. OK. Is there anything else that you'd like to say?

Defendant Bank: Also with the manual modification, once again, the agreement did go out to the borrower with terms on the agreement proposing a modification to be fixed. Once again, we just never got any return from the borrower.

Judge: 'Cause he never got it (laughing).

Defendant Bank: Right.

Expert: Your honor? If I may?

Judge: Yes.

Expert: Uh, the whole program surrounds a 90 day period of time regardless of whether he gets the mail or not. They have no answer in 90 days they're supposed to cancel the program and stop taking the clients money. I mean, that's the thing. He'd been paying for 21 months...

Judge: Oh, that's right!

Expert: ...and they kept taking the money.

Judge: For eighteen months he kept calling and they kept taking the money.

Expert: Kept taking the money.

Judge: Kept asking for more documents.

Expert: Absolutely. That's a typical trait of Bank of America not having enough people to process that. It's like I've been dealing two years with loan modification scammers not having enough process; not enough people to do it.

Judge: So...

Expert: Except they're not...

Judge: Mr. Lopez, uh, so when you sent out that decline letter; it's on the computer so everyone that works there is going to have that information.

Defendant Bank: Yes, your honor.

Judge: So when he calls to make his payments, no, you can't take it... cause you were declined, right?

Defendant Bank: No, your honor. Not necessarily.

Judge: No? (laughs)

Defendant Bank: Payments, when they are called, they go through the home retention division which is our collection line. Even though they are in a workout process for a modification they would still take payments to go towards the obligation loan that the borrower, that the borrower had accepted.

Judge: So he calls and speaks to someone on the phone.

Defendant Bank: Correct, your honor.

Judge: Does he have any proof that he called for every, 18 months? Do you have anything logged in under that?

Defendant Bank: Unfortunately, to navigate the system I need to be hooked up to the server. I have all the screens up as far as the documents that were sent to the homeowner.

Judge: Hmm.

Defendant Bank: As well as documents that were submitted.

Judge: So I guess what I'm saying if he's testifying that he called every month for 18 months and he made telephonic payments you have nothing to help you disprove that. You have nothing to say he didn't do it.

Defendant Bank: Absolutely, your honor. The notes do show that attempts have been made even though he could have called they would just advise me of the notes that we see on our end. People that do take these calls aren't, let's say experienced or certified negotiators. They are collectors.

Judge: So they collect the money but they don't say anything about whether or not there is...

Defendant Bank: They have minimal training in the modification process.

Judge: But they take the money. They have good training about taking money. Right?

Defendant Bank: Yes, your honor.

Judge: Hmm. And they don't have good training on telling them what's on the screen saying you were declined on the 21st of May...a year and a half ago. Correct?

Defendant Bank: I wouldn't be able to speak for them, your honor, but I agree.

Judge: Hmm. OK. That doesn't sound too good. All right. Anything else? Is there anything else you'd like to add Mr. Lopez?

Defendant Bank: No, your honor. That's about it.

Judge: All right. I'll take the matter under submission. Thank you very much. Very interesting.

Expert, Defendant, Plaintiff: Thank you, your honor.

In about 10 days, Dave received a written decision that he had proven his case. The judge awarded him the maximum amount he could under California's small claims limits.

Deciding to Sue Your Bank

As you can see from the transcript, the scene was far from Hollywood. We will go over in greater detail what to say and how to say it-as judges, their expectations, and how they run their courtroom will vary.

Now that you've read what happens in a small claims courtroom, you have to decide if this is right for you. Your bank is *counting* on you <u>not</u> to fight back. They assume that if you are not able to pay your mortgage or have already gone into foreclosure you can't afford to sue them. This book offers a solution that is affordable. It is not just affordability that should help you decide to move forward. You should also ask yourself, and discuss with your family, if you have the *heart* to fight.

The following paragraphs may make you believe I am trying to talk you out of the very plan that I am promoting. In my frank, forthright manner, I want you to be totally prepared for what you may face and the feelings you may have about fighting back. Please know that I am *not* trying to talk you out of this. I am merely pointing out some emotional feelings you may experience.

Many people who are not courtroom veterans do not realize that the only thing you will get out of this exercise is money (and a restored credit score). Many homeowners are so emotionally destroyed by what this ordeal has done to their finances, their health, possibly their marriage, and their children, that all they want is revenge.

Should you successfully sue your bank, the only thing you will be awarded is money. The legal system refers to this as "damages."

Money is the equalizer in the legal system. You will not win an apology. You will not get your health back if this situation has caused you to suffer a health crisis or emotional setback. Your marriage, if it suffered, will not be repaired by suing your bank (though a win may give you some confidence). You will not put the bank out of business. You will not see them led off in handcuffs. *You will receive only money* (and possibly your credit repaired). You have to make peace with this. If you win, the court punishes the bank by awarding you money. Their life will go on and so will yours.

I would like to revisit the Ralph Nader quote that I placed in the front of this book:

"If a million consumers filed a million small claims court actions a year against the banks, the banks would either try to abolish the small claims court or improve their performance."

I cannot give you an exact date when Mr. Nader first said this quote, but he is featured saying it in a Current TV video.[16]

He was not referring to my proposed plan of action. He was referring to banking fees and services. His point however, is correct. If all of the millions of homeowners took a stand and sued their bank-even in small claims court-change would happen. It was estimated by some reports that over 6 million homeowners will faced foreclosure in 2012. In 2013 there are almost 6 million homes *still* facing the possibility of foreclosure. These homeowners face the byproducts of predatory lending practices committed within the past five years by the banks. There are approximately 4 million (or more) homeowners that have been foreclosed on since 2007. If all these homeowners filed the court system would be overwhelmed and real change could occur. Just something to consider as many people ask me what they can do to change things.

---

[16] http://current.com/shows/max-and-jason-still-up/88849140_how-to-beat-the-bank.htm

Another issue in deciding if you want to pursue this, is if you have the time. You will be learning a new skill. You will have to do a lot of reading. I also strongly suggest that you visit your local courtroom two (or more) times and observe so that your fear of the unknown will go away. I have had some clients that skip this step and when their "big day" arrives they were paralyzed with nervousness and just not ready. You need to see what you are up against.

You will need to go through your documents. This act alone may make you angry. If you do get mad, you can use that to your benefit. Getting angry can be very motivating. Anger can also cause you to remember unpleasant things. Have you ever been in a strong argument with a significant other? It's amazing the things you are able to remember. Irritating things that they said or did *years ago* will come to the surface-it is the same with the bank. You will be amazed how strong your memory becomes when you are angry! Use this anger to your benefit. Write down everything you remember. Your memory will be one of the first steps in building your case. Summon this anger the day you go to court!

What if I Can't Afford to Sue my Bank?

Depending on your state, there are avenues you can take if you cannot afford court fees-even in small claims. I will go into what these are called so you know what to ask for or where to look in your state's specific court information.

Search online for the following terms-or ask your local court clerk (it will be called one of the following in your state):

* Fee waiver

* Poverty Affidavit

* *In Forma Pauperis*

* IFP Affidavit (IFP= *in forma pauperis*)

* Pauper's Affidavit

* Fee for Assistance

In some jurisdictions this will be a simple form. In others you will have to make a statement about your finances (a statement is called an Affidavit). In an affidavit you take an oath that what you have written is true. You may have to provide evidence of your financial situation, such as unemployment stubs, disability payments, etc to back up your claims of financial hardship.

Regarding other incidental fees, such as photocopying, perhaps hiring an expert, etc. you may have to pay these fees up front. If you win, ask the judge to order the bank to reimburse you (*do not forget this step*). There are some things you can not be reimbursed for and this will be different in each state. For example, in most states, you cannot sue for lost wages because you had to go to court- particularly if court was your idea.

Please be sure to read my own experiences regarding experts in the small claims courtroom as this <u>can be</u> an added expense (keep reading). I will go over this in more detail. If you are very low on funds to pursue this action, I do not want you to be caught "blindsided" if the judge wants you to have an expert.

For additional low cost or free help visit the back of this book.

Issues to Consider before Diving In

* In all 50 states you will fill in forms. You will not have to draft a 50 page legal motion. Looking at the form will help you begin to formulate your story. The key is to *be brief* on the form. In the court you can go into slightly more detail.

* **NOTE:** In <u>some</u> jurisdictions, *you will not be allowed to argue fraud* in small claims court. The purpose of this book is to educate you *before* you get there and help you decide if small claims is for you. If you live in a jurisdiction where you cannot argue fraud in small claims court, you will have to file your claim in a higher court.

* The judge will not expect you to have gone to law school so there is no need to act like a lawyer.

* Small claims does not take very long. You will likely have a court date 1-3 months after you file your paperwork.

- You will have a lot to read and learn. Expect to give at least 20-30 hours (or more depending on your study and learning habits) on this new project to prepare well. This means consulting sources besides just this book. Read and re-read what you do not understand.

- Review your state's Statute of Limitations[17] rules involving contracts. This is the amount of time you have to file a lawsuit. If you are "cutting it close" in the time limit, you can claim that you did not realize you were a victim of fraud until X date-that is the date the statute starts "ticking." This is perfectly legal. Read more about Statute of Limitations to be sure you understand. If you are suing after the Statute limit, the bank could ask that your case is dismissed.

---

[17] Statutes of Limitations by State: http://www.nolo.com/legal-encyclopedia/statute-of-limitations-state-laws-chart-29941.html

• Find out if your state wants you to try mediation before going to court. Some courts want you to mediate the day of court. Find out what your court wants. The court clerk may have the answer to this-or you may find the answer online. Also know that even if your state does not mention mediation, this may be the way a particular judge runs *his* courtroom. Be sure to observe if this is the case on the days you see how the judge runs his court.

• Are you able to make a 10-15 minute presentation in front of other people? Public speaking is a big fear with many people. Before you answer, consider this: the majority of the people in the room will see your back. In most cases, they are too concerned with what they are about to argue *in their own case* than to worry about you. The person you really have to present to is the judge. In most cases, you will not be speaking for the full 15 minutes. You will likely speak for 20 seconds and then answer questions-just like Dave in his court transcript.

- If it is asked of you, are you able to prove all *the key elements* of your claim? (we will go over this in more detail). This does not mean *all the elements*-just the key ones. If you are going to a higher court, you may have to prove *all the elements*).

- Because most small claims limits may not be the actual amount you lost (they may be less) it is legal to reduce the amount of the claim so that is not larger than the amount you lost. Asking for less money, especially from a bank will hurt, however, as far as asking for actual damages, you may have to cut the amount to fit in your state's small claims limits. In legal terms this is called "waiving the excess." Why on earth would you want to do this? Because the alternative is all the issues that drive up legal costs that I outlined earlier. The alternative would be to file in a higher court. To help you determine how much to ask, consult the link below [18] and read further along in this book.

---

[18] Nolo link: http://www.nolo.com/legal-encyclopedia/free-books/small-claims-book/chapter4-4.html

- In your case you will have the added aspect of fraud (review the definition): Some state statutes on fraud allow you to ask for more damages than you actually suffered as a punishment to the bank for committing fraud. If the statutes allow, I usually ask for *exemplary* or *punitive* damages if the small claims court will honor this request. *Remember, you do have a monetary limit in small claims court, you cannot go over this limit <u>even if the court grants you more damages due to the fraud judgment.</u>* The judge is limited, by law, to the small claims court limits.

- It is not legal to file *two or more cases until you win the amount you desire in small claims.* For example, if you lost $10,000 and your state's small claims limits are $5,000, you can't sue twice *for the same issue*. <u>You CAN sue **the same bank for different issues** however.</u> Some homeowners have tried *and succeeded* to bring multiple suits against the same bank for different issues or claims. It may be a gray area and one that an attorney in your state may be able to help you navigate. The worst thing that could happen is that the judge will disagree and ask you to either "waive the excess" or go to a higher court. Some states, limit the number or times you can file a suit in small claims each year. Check your court rules and maybe contact your county's bar association for advice.

Going to Small Claims Court

There are many books that are specific to your state in your local libraries and are also available online. It would be impossible for me to prepare you for *every contingency* in *every state* (plus, would you want to read through what happens in the other 49 states?).

If small claims is something you want to pursue, I strongly suggest you start with Nolo's *Everybody's Guide to Small Claims Court* by Ralph Warner. The reason I suggest it is because it is very easy to read. If you can borrow a copy at the library that is even better-not just to save on money-but because *about 1/2 of the book will not be applicable to you.* You will want to read about contract disputes and basic "how-to" information. Much of the book is filled with how to handle disputes with neighbors, dog bite cases-almost every thing that a person can sue in small claims for. This is why I have provided links to parts of the Nolo.com website that are applicable to a contracts dispute as well as direct you to basic information.

I have suggested links below and in the back of the book. To get a *brief overview* of you state's small claims rules visit the link below.[19] Be warned-for some reason some states like to move their information around a lot and some of these links may lead nowhere, which means you may have to do some searching.

To begin to prepare for court, consult the link below.[20] It gives you great advice on how to prepare documents, get constructive criticism and how to cope if the bank lies. This link also suggests contacting a lawyer for help in preparing for court. Many people do not know that you can hire a lawyer for 30 minutes to an hour of their time. Not sure which lawyer to contact? Your local bar association will have a lawyer referral service to provide you with recommendations (search under county bar association or, if you live in a large city, look under your city). If you do decide to consult a lawyer check the link below.[21] Make sure their hourly rate fits your budget.

---

[19] Small Claims Rules by state: http://www.nolo.com/legal-encyclopedia/small-claims-court-in-your-state-31016.html

[20] Nolo advice on how to prepare for court: http://www.nolo.com/legal-encyclopedia/free-books/small-claims-book/chapter13-9.html

[21] Nolo's advice on attorney's fees: http://www.nolo.com/legal-encyclopedia/attorneys-fees-basics-30196.html

Small Claims Court Action Plan: Step-by-Step Guide

So now that I've given you many things to consider, where to find information, and where to go if you can't afford it, let me lay out the step-by-step "recipe" to follow for success-or let's hope that's the outcome. Success is, of course, the goal.

I have presented some things that may seem out of order. Many books recommend that you fill in your forms, serve the bank, etc. I ask you to do some homework *before* you ever fill out a form and get you confident in understanding how to build your argument. The order I have placed here is a suggestion. If you want to perform these items in a different order that is okay-just *be sure not to skip any of the steps.*

1.) Go watch a small claims trial in your community

Go to the small claims court where you plan on arguing your case. This is also where you will file your lawsuit if you have to do it in person (in some jurisdictions you can file online). While judges have to follow certain rules, every judge, in every courtroom runs things slightly differently. Observe how things are done. See what the bailiff does and the court clerk. Observe the dress code. Find out where the bathrooms are because if you get a case of nerves, this information will be helpful.

I want to state how *very* important this step is. So many people skip this step because they find it hard to find the time or believe they already know how the courtroom works. Please do not be under the impression that it is like the courtroom TV shows. In addition to studying strategy, understanding legal concepts, learning how the system works, you must study the judge. It is the judge who will take all your hard work and preparation and make a decision. The decision is the reward so why not figure out how to get that reward?

Some judges want you to just sit there- they don't want you to read anything, make notes, and they certainly do not want you to be texting. Make a good impression and just watch. Some judges will ask what you are doing. Do not be at all intimidated because you have every right to be there even if it is as an audience member. They are usually just curious. Tell them that you are researching how his court is run. Don't be overly chatty about your plans to sue. He will cut you off, as he can not discuss your case with you or even offer you legal advice. He will very possibly be impressed that you took the time to research his court.

Observe, or ask the bailiff, this judge's policy on mediation. Some judges demand that you try to mediate before your trial, while others merely suggest it. Be aware, that your state literature may *suggest* it, but the individual judge may *demand* it. Some small claims books even suggest that you do not "have to," but my advice-if the judge wants it, do it! Go by what the judge wants. The judge will be deciding your case, not the state. Most judges just want to make sure every effort is made to resolve your dispute before they make a final judgment.

Be ready for the possibility, whether observing, or actually there for your trial that the judge may be absent and they will have a *pro tem* judge (also called judge *pro tempore*, or visiting judge). This could be a lawyer who is not usually a judge, but is going to be a judge for the day. In most cases, the bailiff will announce this and will give the litigants the choice to proceed. If the bank wants to proceed and you don't, you can wait until the usual judge returns another day, or vice versa-if one of you says no, you will have to come back when the regular judge is there.

Having said all this, if you did your homework and observed the judge and were comfortable with what you saw, you may want to wait until he returns.

If however, you can no longer wait, not take more time off work, etc. in my experience, I find the *pro tem* is very conscientious and wants to do a great job. They are happy to have the opportunity. Don't let the fact that they don't do this every day sway you from thinking they don't know what they're doing. They went to law school, they understand the law, and they will give you a fair trial. If you want to wait for the regular judge, that's okay too. If you want to wait for the regular judge ask for a "*continuance*" - which means prolonging or postponing to another date.

I want to stress again: *please find the time to do this step.*

2.) Review your mortgage and other documents

Now that you've seen how things are done, let's start building your case. It will not be enough that you just tell your story. You will need to show the judge the documents to back up your story. Your documents and notes will be your evidence. Scrutinize every piece of paper you think will help bolster your claim. Think about the legal theories we touched on in the "typical day at the office" scenario. This will help get you thinking what documents will bolster this argument.

The papers you want to concentrate on are the written correspondence from the bank. Take all of your paperwork and put them in a chronological order as if you are building a time line. Look for acceptance letters for the loan modification program, temporary loan modification payment amounts, demand letters from the credit department while you were in the loan modification program, letters from creditors lowering your credit. etc. Look for anything that supports how they "strung you along" for all those months (or years).

Make copies as these will be your exhibits, also known as your evidence. Exhibits are documents that are entered into evidence that will help the judge make a decision on your case. Streamline your large paper collection with just the ones that support your claim. I know this is not easy when you have so many. Remember you are not building a federal case so don't overwhelm the judge with every piece of paper you have.

You may be asked why you applied for a loan modification. List your reasons why you needed a loan modification. If you have written a hardship letter, list the specific items that you mentioned in the letter.

If your credit was destroyed find the documents that say so. Also, if you recall any conversations with bank reps about this, write it down.

Many of my clients have a phone log with the date and time they called the bank and who they spoke with. Sometimes you only have a first name and a representative identification number. If you have this information put this in chronological order so you can easily find it in the courtroom.

Be sure to have copies for the judge, for yourself, and for the bank. The reason the judge was annoyed with the bank rep in Dave's case is that the bank rep should have been prepared to share documents and information. It is not acceptable to just show your computer screen. It is surprising to me that the judge allowed the bank rep to "get away" with this. However, it is the judge's courtroom and he can use some discretion.

As emotional and as wronged as you feel, you are not expected to argue the *trial of the century*, nor will you have that kind of time, so you won't need to bring every document to court-plus it will cause you to fumble through each file instead of spending the time arguing your case.

3.) Organize: Tips from the Courtroom

Everyone organizes differently but I use a trick lawyers use. Invest in *two* three ring binder notebooks-the kind where you can remove papers and put them back. You will also want section dividers *with labels*. I find it easiest to place *one* document in the divider, a contract, for example, and then label the section divider "contract," etc. This allows you to get to the right document quickly. It probably sounds like a lot of work, however, you do not want to spend time fumbling around when you could be making your case.

Notebook #1 is for mediation. You may want to have documents in this notebook to show the bank representative (or the bank lawyer if they are allowed in your state's small claims). You will want to refer to these documents to negotiate with the bank. This notebook will probably have more documents because you will likely have more time.

Notebook #2 is for court. You will want *just the essentials* because you will not have time to flip through tons of papers. The more documents you have, the more you are inviting the possibility of spending time hunting and less time making your case.

I see so many clients that are so conscientious that they bring every document for fear the judge may ask for it. They spend their time rifling through tons of papers to produce what the judge wants. This makes *them* nervous and *some* judges impatient. Remember the objective-you are arguing a contracts case in a short period of time. Don't let the details make you look crazy, disjointed, nervous and unorganized. A few key documents will be enough to make your case.

NOTE: As I mentioned in step 2, you may have to give copies to the judge so be sure to be ready for that. You will learn this on the day you observe (step 1). In most courts, you will not hand the documents over to the judge directly, nor will you approach the bench (the judge's desk) unless you say, "*Your Honor, may I approach?*" In most courtrooms you will hand the COPY of the document to the bailiff (or sometimes the court clerk) and *they* will hand it to the judge.

He will put this in your file and it will help him make a decision.

It is important to know that there should be no surprises in court-*no smoking gun*-like you see on television. Court is supposed to be a level playing field with neither side having the upper hand. For this reason, you will need to provide the other side with copies of whatever documents you are going to refer to, or present as evidence, in order to make your argument. *Your* copy can be yellow highlighted and have notes on it to help *you*, but your opponent should have a copy (without your notes or highlights). You may also need to provide the judge with a copy. (3 copies total: you, the bank, and the judge.)

When you make copies, be sure to get receipts so that if you win, you will be able to ask the judge to rule that the bank reimburse you for all those copies and supplies.

4.) Hiring an Expert

Part of organizing your case is to *consider* hiring an expert. You do not have to hire me. If you know a banking or real estate professional that you trust, you can hire that person-just be sure they can testify to the fraud elements of your case.

It is not absolutely necessary that you hire an expert. As you read in Dave's court transcript, while I provided some assistance when the judge didn't quite "get the whole picture," you can say what I said to make your point. I just reiterated that whatever the bank was doing, they *kept taking the money.* I truly believe no one can tell your story better than you. You lived this! You now know what to say and you can do it! Learn from Dave's experience in court.

Having said that, be warned that *some* judges will want to hear from an expert before they decide if the bank committed fraud and award damages. Some judges are always concerned about their decision getting appealed-an appeal means the judge may have to revisit, or defend his original decision. To avoid this, he wants to get his decision right the first time and may rely on an expert's opinion. To defray your costs, as I stated, you may have to pay an expert for their services however, you can get reimbursed for this cost *if you win.* You must remember to ask to be reimbursed if you win. If you do not win, in most states you will not get reimbursed. The judge will not remember this for you. Get a receipt for the cost of the expert. Have a copy of this receipt in the papers you present to the judge (plus copies of receipts for your other expenses).

It is also not necessary that the expert is there *in person*. An expert can look at your evidence way before your court date and write a report-usually called a declaration or *affidavit* on their findings. They can also testify by telephone-just ask your court clerk if they can make those kind of arrangements.

I mentioned earlier that while it is not absolutely necessary to hire an expert witness, this is what *could* happen: you get there, start testifying, and the judge will stop you and ask if you have an expert. This does not happen *every time* and, of course, I can't predict how *every judge* will act, but be open to the possibility that it *could* happen. This is one of the reasons I strongly encourage you to visit court on at least two days and observe the judge's habits. If this happens, ask for a continuance.

The function of an expert is to help judges understand the evidence. In the legal field, an expert is needed "if the subject matter of your claim requires *specialized knowledge* that is beyond the everyday experience of the average judge." So what does this mean to you? The judge, of course, will understand the basic concept of breach of contract and also of fraud. He may not be very familiar with H.A.M.P. issues. Because of this you may want to consider hiring an expert to look over your documents. I am, of course, available for hire and my contact information can be found near the end of this book.

We talked about a level playing field. Just because you have (or don't have) an expert, does not mean the bank has to produce their own expert to dispute your claim-they can, but it is not usual. They usually have a bank representative who may be seeing your mortgage file for the first time and may never have spoken with you at all. It is up to that bank rep to study your case, dispute your claims, and be prepared for court. They are not the ones who have anything to prove-they just have to defend *your* claims. In other words, the bank does not have the burden of proof, they just have to dispute what you say. In my experience, many times they don't have a lot they can dispute. Read over Dave's courtroom transcript and you will see what I mean.

If you decide to use an expert, be sure you ask for a copy of his resume. The judge may want to know his qualifications.

5.) Considering Mediation

Not every state will offer or suggest mediation. In some states it is "suggested"- usually strongly. This is because small claims court is fast. The judge wants to give you one more try to work it out. I ask you, as much as you may despise your bank, try it. Let the bank rep. see you face-to-face. Let them see you as a real human.

You should absolutely try mediation as this is where the bank *could* offer you a settlement before your small claims trial begins. To prepare for this possibility, I suggest you check out this link from Nolo.com. [22]

The mediators are professionally trained (they are sometimes retired judges and lawyers) and it is their role to facilitate discussion, help you both focus on the issues (not the emotions) and help you both work on a settlement.

The mediator has no power to impose a settlement or a judgement. Make sure you prepare for the possibility of mediation and go in there knowing what you want. A "wait

---

[22] Nolo's Settlement Tips: http://www.nolo.com/legal-encyclopedia/free-books/small-claims-book/chapter6-5.html

and see" approach will not be a good thing as you will find that you are not prepared. Read up on how mediation works. Here are some suggested guidelines to follow:

1.) Think in advance what outcomes you would like and make notes. The mediator may suggest outcomes you have not considered. Keep an open mind but go in knowing what you would like the outcome to be. You may not get everything you want so be open to that possibility.

2.) Bring documents supporting your claim. Even though you are not actually trying the case in mediation, your documents will show the bank what you prepare to ask for. The documents will also help bolster your argument.

3.) The goal behind mediation is not to produce a winner and a loser-it is to reach a compromise.

A very good book to prepare for the possibility of negotiating is *Getting to Yes: Negotiating without Giving In* by William Ury and Roger Fisher. I would also recommend *Getting Past No: Negotiating in Difficult Situations* by the same author. It is a book used in law schools, paralegal training, in many college courses and is even read by diplomats. It is popular so you may be able to find it in your library. If the battle with your bank has been unpleasant *before you arrived in court* it may be worth reading to prepare for the possibility of mediation. If your court does not have mediation available, you may want to contact your court clerk and local bar association to see if these services are available and if there is a cost.

Arranging a mediation may help you get what you want from your bank without going to court. "In person" always seems to get more done than over the telephone where the bank employee perceives you as a faceless customer.

Be open minded. You may have gotten no where with the bank employee sitting in their cubicle and find that you have better luck forcing the bank to face you and negotiate. Many of my clients are very surprised when the bank offers something to settle this matter. You may even receive a phone call from the bank before court offering you a settlement. If this happens, you can think about what you want, discuss it with your family, and call them back. *You do not have to negotiate with them on the spot.* Be prepared for that possibility-particularly if your court wants you to go to mediation first.

You can even go to mediation, negotiate with your bank, and when you are before the judge ask for a continuance. Many judges are extremely happy to agree to give you more time to work things out.

To read more mediation visit the link below.[23]

6.) Legal Research

The only way you will have success in small claims is to have your evidence presented in a manner that will support your claim of fraud against the bank. This will involve some legal research.

One component of gathering your evidence will be to look up your state's statutes for fraud, especially fraud and contracts. Finding the law will include searching your state statutes (laws). Every state has a civil code for fraud. Make a copy of this-it may be lengthy-and review it. Find the section that is applicable to your case such as fraud and contracts. Read the following suggested statement (below) that you can consider using in court. I provide it as a guide-you do not have to use these

---

[23] Nolo's Mediation Tips: http://www.nolo.com/legal-encyclopedia/mediate-small-claims-case-29998.html

words exactly. It will point you in the right direction of what sections of your civil code are applicable to this statement.

When you make your argument for fraud, a suggested way to make your opening statement is as follows:

"Your Honor, Bank of X committed fraud against me in violation of {your state] Civil Code § 1565- 1590 (§ means section) by suppressing the fact that I did not qualify for a loan modification. Bank of X used "undue influence" in getting me to pay a temporary loan modification payment to benefit the bank with prior knowledge that this money would only be used for property taxes and insurance on the property."

This, no doubt, may not sound like the way you would actually speak. The above is a suggestion. I have other suggested phrases in section #7 as well. After you make your initial statement, there will be a question and answer between you and the judge. My advice is to build on one opening "speech" and practice it. Study what was said in Dave's case to get the idea. From there, as in Dave's case, the judge will most likely question you about your claim.

Be aware, that I placed Dave's transcript in here as a guide. Everyone's communication style is different-including the judge. Get *idea*s from my suggestions, but make the statement your own. You noticed in Dave's case there was very little mention of statutes and concepts-just the facts. Other judges will be different-another reason why it is so important to observe.

The purpose of looking up your state statutes on fraud is so that you are prepared to cite the civil code to the judge. He can look it up himself but you are the one making a claim so he will expect that *you* have done this. This shows you have prepared, researched, you know your rights, and you know what you are talking about.

I recommend the following websites below to help you prepare your case. I am not a lawyer so I do not employ fancy methods to find my information when I look up statutes. You will not be expected to either.

Doing legal research can sometimes be overwhelming. You have likely been through a lot and your attention span may not be in sync for what is required to look up this information. You may want to ask a law student or paralegal student for help. Offer to buy them lunch or coffee in exchange for their help. Many are very flattered you asked for their help and are just "chomping at the bit" to help people. You could even post a memo on a local law or paralegal school bulletin board asking someone to help you with this task.

Before hiring anyone, or just "asking" someone, have a look around the websites below and see what *you* find:

1.) Visit Justia [24] and type the search terms you are looking for in the search box at the top of the page (and be sure to type in your state).

2.) Visit Google Scholar[25] and *be sure to check the box for legal documents.*

3.) Cornell University.[26] I know what you've seen on television. The actors who are playing lawyers are citing cases left and right (*Brown vs. Board of Education,* for example). You will not have to do this. This site is suggested for basic information you may want to look up.

---

[24] http://www.justia.com

[25] http://scholar.google.com/schhp?hl=en

[26] http://www.lawschool.cornell.edu/library/WhatWeDo/ResearchGuides/Basics.cfm

I want you to warn you not to over prepare and look up every conceivable statute and law and go in to court with a stack of printed stuff. You will not have time to search through this stack during your court appearance. Also, this is Small Claims court. As I have mentioned on several occasions, the judge does not expect you to have studied law. Your issue is a simple contract dispute with the added element of fraud. Even if your state allows lawyers in the small claims courtroom that does not mean that the judge expects *you* to have stuffed in 3 years of law school before your 20 minute appearance.

7.) Understanding your argument

In this section I am going to review concepts that we talked about in our "typical day at the office" scenario. I have no doubt that the concepts you are about to read will have your head spinning. The reason for this is that they are all intertwined and have same, or similar meanings. I am not AT ALL suggesting that you be able to recite each definition. *PLEASE* do not do this! I have placed these here to arm you with information and give you confidence that you are on the right track in pursuing fraud.

As you saw from Dave's small claims transcript, legal definitions were not cited however the *concepts* of those definitions were intertwined with what Dave was asking from the court. Let's review Dave's opening statement to the judge:

Plaintiff Dave: Your honor, I feel that I was taken unfair advantage of by the defendants when they approached me with the purpose of involving me in a home loan modification under the H.A.M.P. program. Under the guidelines of that program my monthly mortgage would not have been able to exceed 31% of my monthly gross income.

Further on, Dave states:

Plaintiff Dave: They told me that because of the type of loan that I had that I was eligible to apply for this mortgage modification and that it would take approximately 90 days to get an answer whether I'd get it or not. That I would qualify. [27]

Plaintiff Dave : Uh, well, we proceeded to agree upon a reduced monthly mortgage

---

[27] *This is where Dave is building his case stating that he believed what the bank said (relied on the bank to his detriment) and they strung him along to get more money out of him (knowing misrepresentation of the truth-see fraud definition on the next page).* To review, as part of H.A.M.P. guidelines, Dave was supposed to receive an answer "yeah" or "nay" in 3 months. If you are like Dave, they strung you along too.

amount. They reduced my mortgage by $400.00 a month during this trial period which was supposed to be about 90 days, during which they requested more information which had been sent already. They said they did not have the information. (*By requesting more information, the bank strung Dave along in an effort to collect money for that escrow account. The longer they strung Dave along, the more money they take*).

Plaintiff Dave: ...I continued to make the forbearance payments on a monthly basis. I chose to do it through the telephone so that I would be in touch with them on a monthly basis. Every month I had asked the representative that I talked to, which was a different one each time, what the progress was, and I was told that my account was still under review and that I should continue to make forbearance payments. This went on for about 18 months. During that 18 month period I received notices from some other creditors stating that they were reducing my credit amount due to some reported late mortgage payments. And when I contacted, I believe it was BAC (Bank of America Credit) Loan Servicing they had explained to me that because there was a difference between what I was paying and what I was contracted to pay under my mortgage that they had to report that difference as late mortgage payments. (*Dave is making sure the judge understands how he was strung along in this trial period*).

So here are the concepts we are going to review (but not memorize) to build *your* case:

Fraud

Some of our most important laws deal with fraud and it makes for an unlevel "playing field" and puts one side at a disadvantage over another. Generally speaking, if a transaction is fraudulent, the deal is off.

According to Black's Legal Dictionary, fraud is

- *A knowing misrepresentation of the truth or concealment of a material fact to induce another to act to his or her detriment.*

- *A misrepresentation made recklessly without belief in its truth to induce another person to act.*

- *A tort arising from a knowing misrepresentation, concealment of material fact, or reckless misrepresentation made to induce*

another to act to his or her detriment.

• ***Unconscionable dealing, especially in contract law, the unconscientious use of the power arising of the parties relative positions and resulting in an unconscionable bargain.***

If you were to read more on fraud in Black's legal dictionary (a dictionary that many judges, lawyers, students, law professors and scholars consult) the various definitions go on for several pages (in very small print). You will find Black's Law Dictionary in any medium to large sized library. However, I *do not* ask you to be familiar with the 24+ types of fraud. You are arguing the bank was fraudulent in contract fraud and that you relied to your *detriment* on their promise-their stringing you along to get more money out of you.

• **Fraud in the inducement:** Fraud occurring when a misrepresentation leads another to enter into a transaction with a false impression of the risks, duties, or obligations involved; an intentional misrepresentation of a material risk or duty reasonably relied on, thereby injuring the other party without vitiating[28] the contract itself, especially about a fact relating to value.

* **Intentional Misrepresentation**: The act of making a false or misleading statement about something, usually with the intent to deceive. A statement that does not accord with the facts.

* **Negligent Misrepresentation:** A careless or inadvertent false statement in circumstances where care should have been taken.

* **Fraudulent Concealment**: The affirmative suppression or hiding, with the intent to deceive or defraud, of a material fact or circumstance that one is legally bound to reveal. Hiding a key fact.

* **False Promise**: A promise with no intention of carrying it out.

---

[28] When you vitiate a contract you destroy the legal effect of it.

Elements of Fraud

Depending on the legal dictionary you review, fraud can have 5-7 elements. If you are planning to argue fraud *in a higher court* you *may* have to prove ALL of the elements. This is small claims. You **do not** have to go into that kind of detail. I mention them to get you thinking that you are on the right track in formulating and arguing your fraud claim. If all these issues happened, you have a strong claim of fraud.

Here are the elements to concern yourself with in formulating your argument:

- It was a false statement

- The statement substantially affected your ability to make a decision to enter into a contract or make plans (such as walk away from your home, do a short sale, etc.)

- The bank knew the statement to be true

- The false statement was made with the intent to deprive you of your rights (to make plans, etc).

- You could not rely on the statement because it was false.

• The statement caused you damage. (You lost money, your home, etc.)

Detrimental Reliance

Detrimental Reliance: Reliance by one party on the acts or representations of another, causing a worsening of the first party's position. Detrimental reliance may serve as a substitute for consideration (exchange of money) and thus make a promise enforceable as a contract. See promissory estoppel. (*from Black's Law Dictionary*)

Promissory Estoppel

To review, promissory estoppel means that you relied on the bank's promise as they strung you along.

<u>Three elements</u> should be in place to prove promissory estoppel.

1. The one who made the promise (the bank) makes a gratuitous promise to induce *an action* to the person being promised-you, the homeowner (*the action* is paying your mortgage).

2. You act on that promise-at a substantial detriment, an economic loss.

3.   Injustice could have been avoided if only the promise was enforced (if you received the loan modification you would not have lost your home).

Promissory Estoppel: The principle that a promise made without consideration may nonetheless be enforced to prevent injustice if the promisor (the bank) should have reasonably expected the promise (the homeowner) to rely on the promise and if the promisee did actually rely on the promise to his or her detriment. Also termed <u>inaccurately</u> *equitable estoppel.*

Equitable Estoppel: (1) A defensive doctrine preventing one party from taking unfair advantage of another when, through false language or conduct, the person to be estopped has induced another person to act in a certain way, with the result that the other person has been injured in some way. This doctrine is founded on principles of fraud.   The five essential elements for this type of estoppel are (a) that there was a false representation or concealment of material facts, (b) that the representation must have been known to be false by the party making it, or the party must have been negligent in not knowing its falsity, (c) that it was believed to be true by the person to whom it was made, (d) that the party making the representation must have intended that it be acted on, or the person acting on it must have been justified in assuming this intent, and (e) that the party asserting estoppel acted on the representation in a way that will result in a substantial prejudice unless the claim of estoppel succeeds. Also termed *estoppel by conduct*; *estoppel in pais* (2) See *promissory estoppel*.

Undue Influence

I mentioned this term when I offered a suggestion of what to say in court under the legal research section. Undue influence is a term I sometimes use. It is a suggestion if you want to use it. Essentially it means that the bank is using its power of promising you a loan modification and by promising things, they are influencing you to do certain things-such as continuing to pay money-again, to string you along. It is a term that is inter-related to the other concepts we discussed.

Undue Influence: (1) The improper use of power or trust in a way that deprives a person of free will and substantiates another's objective. (2) Consent to a contract, transaction, relationship, or conduct that is voidable if the consent is obtained through undue influence.

Verbal Contracts

If you were made promises over the phone, this section will be applicable to you. If this is not the case, skip this section.

Verbal contracts are legal in **SOME** circumstances. There are six circumstances. You will only need to be familiar with TWO circumstances when a verbal contract is NOT valid. You do not necessarily need to recite them to the judge. They are included here for your basic understanding.

The two circumstances applying to your case are (1) issues dealing with real estate and (2) contracts that are worth more than $500. As you can already see, your issue deals with real estate and your house is worth more than $500 so the bank employee should not have made promises (contracts) over the phone.

Statute of Frauds is a concept studied in the first year of law school in the contracts course. *Do not get bogged down in every detail of the six circumstances.* I have boiled it down to the above. When I said in my MSNBC interview that the judge was appalled that this was done over the phone, this concept is why.

It is not important in small claims court that you are able to cite all the reasons when a verbal contract is not a legally binding contract. You can use this as an argument that your verbal contract is not binding for the two reasons cited above and use it as a bargaining tool if you go to a mediator.

For your general information, here is the definition of Statutes of Frauds:

Statute of Frauds: (1) An English statute enacted in 1677 declaring certain contracts judicially unenforceable (but not void) if they are not committed to writing and signed by the party to be charged. The statute was entitled "An Act for the Prevention of Frauds and Perjuries" - also termed Statute of Frauds and Perjuries. (2) A statute (based on the English Statute of Frauds) designed to prevent fraud and perjury requiring that certain contracts be in writing and signed by the party to be charged. Statute of frauds traditionally apply to the following types of contracts:

* **a contract for the sale or transfer in the interest of land (real estate)**;

* a contract that cannot be performed within one year of its making;

- **a contract for the sale of goods valued at \$500 or more;**

- a contract of an executor or administrator to answer for a decedent's debt;

- a contract to guarantee the debt or duty of another;

- a marriage contract.

Boiling it down into workable soundbites

Again, as you read, Dave did not argue complicated legal concepts but he had to understand them to make his argument work in a way the judge could apply the law. Your observation of your judge will help you determine how much detail the judge wants from you. That is exactly why I suggest it as a first step. It may not be necessary to make a grandiose speech, citing state fraud statutes especially if the judge wants something simpler-as was the case with Dave.

Your argument to the court is that the bank had prior knowledge that you were not qualified for a loan modification based on the fact that 31% of your gross income would not support your mortgage payment, taxes, and insurance. You will drive this point home by showing the judge the H.A.M.P. 31% guidelines in the back of this book. Bring copies of these charts to refer to in court.

To press this argument even further, you will present the court with your loan modification denial letter that was sent to you *months or years after* you have been making temporary payments showing that the bank had prior knowledge that you would not qualify. If you received a denial over the phone with no contracts or agreements, state that this was done verbally. The judge knows Statute of Frauds and can apply them without you explaining the concept.

If you feel you have been defrauded, make sure you state this in your opening short statement. The judge may rescind a contract that involves fraudulent conduct and order that your money be refunded, along with any damages you suffered as a result of the fraud (all under your state's small claims limits).

Your opening statement may be something like this: *"Your Honor, the bank strung me along in a trial period that under H.A.M.P. guidelines, should have only lasted 3 months. They had the knowledge that I was not qualified for a loan modification program because the 31% of my income would not support the existing mortgage payment, insurance, and taxes on the home."*

This is where you may want to show the judge the chart from our website.

"The bank keep me in a trial loan modification program beyond the initial three month trial period and led me to believe that I would get a loan modification if I just kept paying. I later learned that the money I paid all those months did not go to pay my mortgage but to an escrow account for the bank to safe guard my home as their asset. The bank now wants me to pay late fees, interest, attorney fees, and administration fees or they will foreclose on my home. As a result of this ordeal, my credit score was ruined and the bank never warned me that this would occur." You may also want to mention your states' civil code, including section of the code to drive home your point. It may be helpful to have a copy of the code with you.

Arguing Personal Injury

A word of warning if you want to argue how hurt, depressed, etc. you are/were as a result of the bank's actions. It can be <u>*extremely difficult*</u> to argue in small claims in addition to your contract claims. You can *try* to argue it as another issue, as I mentioned earlier.

Also, the small claims court amount will probably not be able to compensate you for this. If this is an issue you really want to argue, you may want to consider arguing in a higher court. You will have to prove that the bank's actions were intentional and that this intention caused a medical condition (stroke, depression, etc.) It is a *tough* argument to put on in small claims but *not impossible*. The judge will very possibly ask you to produce medical experts. This may be an added expense for you, but if you argue it successfully, the judge may award you the cost of the experts as part of your damages. Since this is small claims, you can hire a nurse to attest to your medical issues. You could also bring your doctor or a less expensive alternative would be to bring a written declaration.

Review the statement in *"Issues to Consider Before Diving In"* and see if you can file two issues (see the last statement in this section). It may possibly be worth a try-just be able to prove that the bank's actions caused your illness.

8.) Study the video [29]

Many people do not pay full when they watch a news story. You may not think to give it your full attention but if you want to successfully present your case, the video holds *many* clues.

I am providing you with a transcript of the video so you can study it. The reason this is important is that there are *phrases* in there that will help you understand the concepts I have outlined and *why* they are important. Watching the video several times will help you explain *your* issues to the judge, and most importantly **why** you are suing.

I want to point out, that just because Dave had the help of an expert does not mean you have to have an expert. You can study the points I make and state them yourself. Remember-this happened to you and you are the best one to tell your story. I was more help to Dave in the preparation before the trial. His confidence was beaten down and he wanted to be sure he was on the right track. Also, Dave did not have a book to prepare him as you do.

---

[29]http://SueYourBank.com/video

As a side note, allow me to offer you some advice: do not bring this video to court, play it for the judge, and say, *"I want that."* I had a client try that, without explaining *his own story.* His case was dismissed and the judge was annoyed. *You do not want an annoyed judge!*

****

Below is the transcript from the Dylan Ratigan Show appearance. I have placed the important phrases in **bold letters**. If your case is very similar to Dave's you will want to think about how these phrases relate to your own case, and how you will present them to the judge.

The video has closed captioning.[30] If closed captioning is available on your device, you can view it in one of 57 languages by clicking on "CC" at the bottom of the video. The captioning does go by rapidly so feel free to stop the video and slow it down. For some people, reading the closed captioning helps them understand the points made in the video much better.

---

[30] Closed captioning on YouTube may not be available on all devices such as iPads and some cell phones.

Dylan Ratigan: The little guy takes on the big bank and wins? A true David vs. Goliath victory.   In this case the homeowner's name, in fact, is Dave.

It all started when Dave Graham tried to change his loan under the government's Home Affordable Modification Program known as H.A.M.P.   It was a last ditch effort to save his home from foreclosure. **For an 18 month trial period Graham made reduced payments on his mortgage only to find out after having done so from Bank of America that he wasn't going to be considered eligible for the modification that he had been paying for the past year and a half.**

As a result of the reduced payments of course his credit score was wrecked because they retracted the modification but Dave fought back and at the very least won a little money - $7,500 bucks which was the maximum the judge could give him in small claims court.

Dave Graham joins us now, along with Alan Sims, who is the real estate forensic specialist who helped him with his case - think of him as sort of a mortgage "CSI" character.

We reached out to Bank of America about this case and here is their response:

"We were unable to complete a modification under the government's Home Affordable Program because Mr. Graham did not provide all of the documentation required under the federal guidelines. [31]   We have offered, and remain willing to consider Mr. Graham for a modification under proprietary non-government programs, which may allow us more leeway."

Dylan Ratigan: So Dave, in the context of that comment from Bank of America, did you not provide all of the necessary documentation and what did happen from your perspective?

Dave: Well Dylan, **we did comply with their requests for documentation, probably**

---

[31] *Earlier I mentioned that the bank's statement that Dave did not provide all of the documents is an untrue statement. Also, because Dave's credit was destroyed by the 18 month H.A.M.P. ordeal, he would never qualify for a "proprietary non-government program" [he means an in-house bank loan]. If the bank uses this statement during your trial, this will be your argument. The state of your credit after H.A.M.P. is likely like Dave's.*

about three times during this 18 month process. [32]

If there was something that was still missing, I was not made aware of it. In fact, I had actually asked the representatives that I talked to each month while making my payments if there was anything necessary to be sent and they always told me no there was not. They didn't show anything.

Dylan Ratigan: Alan, you say that Bank of America uses the **promise** of this type of a modification basically as a way to milk a little bit more money (*you will explain the money did not go to the principle of your mortgage*) out of somebody who's house they know they're going to foreclose on anyway. So they basically say, "Hey, we'll give you the modification, you give us the dropped payment. They get the extra 18 months worth of money and then they say, hey, guess what, thanks for the money, we're taking your house."

---

[32] *It is important to mention that you did everything the bank asked. This will put to rest the "your word against theirs" argument as you did everything **they asked.***

Alan Sims: Yes, that's true. **They knew within 90 days of this process that Dave didn't qualify for this loan so they kept on taking the money for an additional 18 months after this 90 days.**[33] **They use the money in a escrow account that pays for taxes and insurance first, that doesn't even go towards their mortgage that he needs to reduce.** (*The money _did not go toward your mortgage_ so with all the money you paid for all those months _you did not receive any benefit out of the bargain of this contract_.*)

So it's like subsidizing the bank's inventory so they don't have to pay any insurance or taxes on the property.

Dylan Ratigan: Well Dave, **did they tell you within 90 days that you weren't going to qualify**? (*This is _detrimental reliance_. Stringing the homeowner along, making them believe if they just hang in there, they will get that loan modification but all along the decision makers at the bank knew, or were*

---

[33] *Note that even in Dave's trial, this concept had to be repeated to the judge a few times. Review the "potential new client" conversation at the beginning of this book and the legal concepts I discuss there. Formulate a way to make the concepts "mesh" with _your_ story.*

supposed to know that the homeowner never would qualify).

Dave: No sir-they kept making these trial period payments for 18 months before they actually had told me that I would have to make up that back money of about $7,000 or lose my home.

And, at that point, a little further investigation, I found out that supposedly they had sent notice to me that I did not qualify 3 months prior to that. Of course, I never got that notice. Their response to me when I questioned them was, "Well, did our part. It's not our responsibility if you didn't get it."

Dylan Ratigan: If the banks own the vast majority of the houses in America-which they do. And if the banks don't have any money-which they do not because they get it by the trillion from the federal government and the U.S. taxpayer-so you have this unholy alliance between the tax base and the banking system and the profits from the banking system used to fund the politicians-in order to get the politicians to continue giving the banks the money what recourse do any of us have in the context of a theoretical democracy if the federal government and the mega-banks are in this unholy alliance, Alan? [34]

Alan Sims: It's just dismal and what my, at least my organization tries to do, is we get the homeowner to go ahead and realize that the house, especially in this HA.M.P. program is gonna be lost. They already have you "pegged" as being foreclosed *(I went into this in the section, "Why Would the Bank Want My Home to go into Foreclosure?")* in the future so let's try to attract two issues. Get you a little cash from small claims and the second is try to get your credit repaired with a positive judgement and that's what Dave's going to be faced with because those are the two major issues for the homeowners. "I want to start over again. I want to get off that crazy train I'm on right now. I want my life to go on." So they have to take the responsibility to go ahead and go after the banks. They have to say I've had enough of this type of sham of a loan scam program. I want start my life over again. I want to get my credit repaired. And that's what Dave is really trying to go after.

---

[34] *While this is an interesting question, do not use your time in front of the judge to point out the problems with the system as a whole. Use your time to talk about <u>what happened to you</u> while in this system.*

Dylan Ratigan: And Dave, why do you think the judge ultimately ruled in your favor on this case?

Dave: Well, we were able to produce the evidence necessary to prove that they had prior knowledge that I was not going to qualify. **They actually had promised me things that they could not and were not going to deliver.** (*Detrimental reliance*)

It was a pretty clear cut case that they had pretty much deliberately done wrong.

Dylan Ratigan: Alan, is this the start of a trend? You have a judge here in California who ruled in the little guys favor in the face of what sounds like fairly overwhelming evidence. There was another ruling out of Massachusetts today that was again, against the banks. Is the court, are the judges the last line of defense here and are they actually potentially starting to wake up and smell the coffee as it were?

Alan Sims: Yes they are. Again what we were able to do, especially in this venue-in the small claims venue-is to have the homeowner with the tools I'm able to provide, go in and say, **"Look-I'm a victim of <u>fraud.</u>"**

In California, it's under **specific Civil Code and here's the evidence.** (*We talk about this in the legal research section (#4). When you go before the judge and bring up fraud and be prepared to cite the section number of the fraud statute. Is it not acceptable that you say, "The whole statute, Your Honor."*)

As an expert witness, I give them the tools do this and in Dave's case they were **covering up** (*fraud*) information-the Bank of America was- before and during this period of time and they also had undue influence to go ahead and take advantage of Dave so that he would make some decisions.

All of this was done **without contracts.** [35] **They did it over the phone** and the judge was appalled with that. Also-that was the main thing and this happens to millions of people nationwide.

Dylan Ratigan: Listen. Thank you both for sharing your story with us and kudos to both of you for again, turning your wishes into a goal, making a plan, and executing it.

---

[35] *Statute of Frauds.*

9.) Figuring out your damages-how much to sue for

Some states will want to know this on the form while others will wait until the trial day to "hash" that out.   If you live in a state where they want to know the amount up front, and then when you get to court, you somehow uncover other matters and want *more* money, you can either file an amended form or state it in court-what the correct procedure is depends on your state rules. Please read up on your state's rules on this.

Figuring damages may be one of the more important parts of your case.   You will be figuring out how much money to ask the judge to award you if you win your case.

H.A.M.P. is designed to assist the homeowner in saving their home from foreclosure by offering you reduced mortgage payments. The program has specific guidelines that tell the bank a time table to process your information and let you know if your are eligible.

The most important guideline is the 90 days that the bank has to put you in a temporary loan modification.   Many of my clients are in "temporary limbo" for *well over* 90 days-some as long as two years. The "how long" will be factored in as part of your damages.

In the case of damages, the analysis must be done on your original qualification for the program. We start with the 31% test. In the back of this book I have devised a table called *Affordability Index Making Home Affordable Plan Chart*[36] that you can find in the back of this book. Since you may need to print it out to show the judge, follow the instructions in the back of the book.

This calculation is started by taking 31% of your gross income (what you make *before* taxes are taken out). This dollar amount has to support your mortgage payment, property taxes, and insurance on your home. That amount is the new loan modification payment.

The bank has 90 days to make a decision on your permanent loan modification. If you do not qualify, than the bank is supposed to offer you the options of a short sale or deed in lieu of foreclosure.

The damage aspect of your case is based on the continual payment to the bank that goes beyond the 90 day trial period.

---

[36] http://courtroom-advocates.com/mha-docs.pdf

One example of basic damages is the trial payment you made to the bank over the 90 day period. If your were never qualified for a loan modification, why did the bank keep taking your money?

Let say, for example, that you have paid $1,500.00 in temporary loan modification payments for the past 12 months. You were just told by the bank you do not qualify and they are going to foreclosure on your home.

- Your damages are calculated by multiplying $1,500 monthly x 12 = $18,000.00.

- Now you are going to subtract the 90 days that the bank has to qualify your loan modification program. $1,500.00 month x 3 = $4,500.00.

- Then the damages are $18,000.00 - $4,500.00 = $13,500.00.

- If you live in California, for example, and the small claims court limit is $10,000, you will have to "waive the excess," and even though your damages are $13,5000, you can only ask to be awarded $10,000 (unless you go to a higher court).

Other Damages (non-money damages)

There are other damages that you should consider, called *punitive damages*. See the back of this book for a full definition.

If your case resembles Dave's, your bank did not warn you that your credit would affected when agreed to H.A.M.P.

You will need to explain to the judge *one* of the following scenarios:

1.) You were current on your mortgage before you entered into H.A.M.P. and after being in the program your credit score was adversely affected, or

2.) You were missing mortgage payments and they advised you to try H.A.M.P., and being in the program made your credit score even worse, or

3.) The bank told you to deliberately miss mortgage payments before you could be eligible for H.A.M.P., and then being in H.A.M.P. made your credit score even worse.

If your case resembles Dave's (and the millions of other people who were, or are in H.A.M.P.), your bank did not warn you that your credit would affected when entered into H.A.M.P.

Important: If you meet any of these criteria, ask the judge to order that your credit be corrected because of their deceptive practices as part of your damages.

10.) Figuring out *who* to sue

You will most likely be suing your bank-which is a corporation-so you will be suing a business entity (not the people). You do not have a claim against the employees, or even the owners of the bank. You need to know this to make sure your small claims form is filled out correctly. Your case will be dismissed if it is incorrect. Your form should not list any people. You can *send the form with an address to* a specific person, but the actual court form should *only list the bank* as a corporation.

You will want to check with your Secretary of State to know where to serve the form. Many courts will allow your form to be "served" by mail. By checking with the Secretary of State (usually on their website), you will be able to find the address of where to send your complaint, or court form. Search on the Secretary of State website for some of the following terms: corporations, business entities, service of process, substituted service of process. On this site, the corporation designates an "agent for service of process" or where they want to receive documents when they are being sued. Expect this site, in most cases, to be jam packed and confusing. You can do this. If you get no where, call your bank and ask them where to send court papers.

Even if your bank is headquartered in another state, you can still sue. The rules are that you can sue any business that is organized (meaning incorporated or an LLC [Limited Liability Corporation]) in your state if they have a piece of real estate in your state (branch office, warehouse, etc.-*even if the headquarters is in another state*).

Some may advise you that you cannot sue if the bank is headquartered in another state-*this is <u>not</u> true.* The courts will allow you to sue if:

* The bank provides services in your state.

* Calls you in your state and talks about banking business (such as your mortgage).

* Sends you mail.

* Solicits you online or in an email.

- The bank advertises in your state's media (newspapers, magazines, billboards, etc.)

You can also sue where the contract was carried out and signed. The bank can also be sued "where they failed to keep their bargain"-that would be your house.

11.) Court documents

Depending on how procedures are done in your state, you can file in person, by fax, mail or online. Pay attention to what forms you need and follow your state's procedure to the letter.

You should receive a court date when you file. If you find out later that the date is not convenient, review your courts rules on how this is handled.

Each state has their own system. Some states, such as New York, have a sub-system which means they want you to follow state guidelines, but also the guidelines in your municipality. The majority of the courts call it a Plaintiff's Claim or Form. Start looking the form over and formulate what you want to say.

You will notice that the form has a *very* small space to state why you are suing. This is for a reason-they want you to get to the point. *This is not the place to try your case.* Write a few practice statements before you actually put it on the form. Do this in a clinical, non-emotional way-just the facts.

When you actually get to court, the bailiff, court clerk, or judge may read it to get a "handle" on the nature of your complaint. Once he reads it, he will then give you a chance to elaborate-that is when you try your case. My point is again-do not try the case on the form. You are understandably emotional and you want every chance to "tell them off"-don't. As they say to actors, save it for the camera (that is, save it for your day in court).

Also almost every state has the forms available on line and well, some do a better job of it than others in helping you to find it. You may find in your search that some of the links don't work. It can be frustrating. You must persist.

We live in a capitalist country. Many web "entrepreneurs" know you are looking for this information, they know the "state" of your state's website, and will very possibly be some of the first websites you find on your search.   This is because they are better at search engine optimization than your state probably is.   You are welcome to use these sites but while they may appear free at first, many are not.   They are counting on your state's site being confusing so they want you to pay a small fee on *their* site.   Finding the right forms and information may take a little digging so do not be tempted to fall into the first site you see. Look for websites that end in ".gov" and that should give you a clue that you are on a state website.

A word about **demand letters**-practically every book, website, and advice area will advise you to write a demand letter. You can write a letter or make a phone call (just be sure to document the date you did this in your notes and whom you spoke with). Some judges may ask if you contacted the bank prior to filing your lawsuit.   Some will not.

Court Clerks: With many forms and information online you may have very limited dealing with court clerks.   In some states, they want you to do things "the old fashioned way" which means standing in line, filing your forms, and getting your court date.

I have been in many courts. Some court clerks are extremely helpful and some go out of there way not to.   Be ready for this possibility so you can be ready but not in a "tell them off" and argue way-just know what to expect. Be aware that like many government agencies (and even private businesses) that everyone is cutting back on staff and this may cause an air of "grumpiness." Even every self-help court book will warn you of this. Being "less than helpful" seems pervasive around the nation. Thank goodness you can now find most of your answers online. My advice is to start there by gathering all your information, observing your local court to see how things are done, and rely on the court clerks to "fill in the blanks" on issues you cannot find elsewhere.

When you deal with the clerks, be respectful as you would with any other human you want something from. They are there to help you.

Filing more than one case to get more money: I mentioned this earlier, but to review- If you want to sue your bank for $20,000 and your state limits are only $10,000, for example, it is *not* legal to split your case into pieces to make it fit *for the same* issue. What is legal is suing the same bank for *multiple issues*. It is tricky, but can be done.   As long as each suit states a different claim, it is acceptable. This concept may take some thought and creativity on your part. If this is an option you feel you can try, be aware that certain states have rules about how many small claims suits you can bring in a year's period of time. Review your state's rules on this.

12.) Serving court papers

I will not go into great detail here. Check your court rules and any books you are reading on small claims court. Be sure to observe any time limits for serving the papers. "Serving the papers" means notifying the bank that you are suing them.

13.) Practice, practice, practice

Need I say more?   You know yourself better than I. Practice what you will say until it is second nature. Imagine you see an old friend in a elevator and you have just the elevator ride to tell her what happened with your bank. Say it just as if you were telling a friend but you have to "cut to the chase" and get to the heart of the matter.

If you are one who lets your nerves get the better of you, may I suggest looking at hypnosis tapes to help you relax.   There are several to choose from and they are very inexpensive and some are free. Use headphones to listen while you relax. I am not a hypnosis expert, but from my experience, for hypnosis to take effect, you will need to listen to it 21 days in a row. I do not recommend waiting until you are on your way to the courthouse to start listening.

14.) Get ready for court

You've already practiced, did all your homework. Take a deep breath and get ready to take on the bank!

Leave the Nolo books and law dictionary at home. Remember Dave's experience. Dave did not have time to flip through a book to make his point. He did not have this book to help him or previous experience as this was the first case of it's kind. Benefit from Dave's experience and use it to your advantage.

- <u>Eat</u>: This is not the time to have low blood sugar.

- <u>Bring a working pen:</u> for obvious reasons. Take notes when you are in mediation.

- <u>Silence that Cell Phone:</u> Don't you hate it when someone's cell phone goes off in an inappropriate place? Magnify that by 1000 and that's how the judge feels too. Also, most judges do not like it when you are texting and fooling with your phone while you wait your turn. Out of sight and OFF is the best advice.

- <u>Bring Cash:</u> Many courtroom parking lots are in a municipal paid lot. Be prepared.

- <u>Entourage:</u> You may want to bring a friend for moral support. That is entirely up to you. If you have a chatty friend, I would leave them at home. *You will want to focus and concentrate.* For this reason, make every attempt to find a baby sitter if you have young children. Some parents have no choice but to bring their children with them. If that is the case, try to hire a baby sitter to play with them outside until you are done. You don't want to be distracted. You don't want the judge to be distracted either.

- H.A.M.P. Chart: This chart I made for Dave and my other clients.[37] If you are reading this book from an eReader that will not allow you to print, not to worry.

- State Statue or Civil Code if you plan on referring to it.

- Your Two Trial Notebooks with the documents

- Copies for the judge and the bank

- Expert Declaration: if you hired an expert.

15.) The verdict

As I have stated many times, all courts run differently. Sometimes you will get an answer right there. Sometimes the judge wants to review all the documents, perhaps the testimony (if it is recorded) and mail you a decision. If you have questions about this procedure, ask the court clerk or consult your state's website on small claims matters.

Depending on your jurisdiction, you will have an answer one way or another in a matter of several days or weeks.

---

[37] http://courtroom-advocates.com/mha-docs.pdf

Alan R. Sims

What if I Want to Try a Higher Court?

If you can afford the time and the money to invest in a higher court you should look into it. The theories I have discussed can work in higher courts. (*Please review my disclaimer at the beginning of this book*). I strongly recommend Nolo's *Represent Yourself in Court: How to Prepare & Try a Winning Case* by attorneys Paul Bergman and Sara Berman-Barrett. Invest in the newest edition you can find (at the date of this publication, that would be the 7th edition). I suggest many Nolo books on my website. They are well written and very easy to understand. If you visit Nolo.com you will receive updates on the latest information about your legal topic.

Choices

I wanted to say some final words-particularly to those skeptics out there. You may also have seen media reports telling you not to bother suing your bank.

I am not a preacher, therapist, or spiritual leader. In fact, as I receive phone calls from all over the nation by women, and even men in tears, it is hard to be spiritual. In a nation such as this, these stories are not supposed to happen from people who worked hard, played by the rules and wanted to be part of the American dream. It is an unbelievable state we find ourselves in and as you look around, I'm sure you will admit that even the greatest financial minds offer little to few solutions.

I *do* know that when things go bad in life we have really only two choices:

Give up, or

Move on

To some of you I imagine the plan in the book I have outlined is completely unacceptable. You have suffered way too much, lost too much, maybe even cried too much to accept a small amount of money from small claims court while the bank is not only rolling in their own money, but in tax payer money from bailouts. If you are outraged, I really don't blame you. It is hard to swallow that as the richest, most powerful, and most resourceful nation on earth this situation has left us with so few choices.

Give up, or

Move on

If you choose option number one, give up, I offer no judgment on you. Sometimes the situations life hands us seem so insurmountable, giving up seems like the easiest of the two.

If you choose option number 2, move on, I ask you to not only fight back, but ask your friends and neighbors to join you. Offer support to each other. Teach each other what you have learned in this book and from other sources. Lean on each other. The one thing that built America is our ability to take action and combine our resources for results. *Action changes things*. It built this country. Your action can overwhelm the court system. When a system is overwhelmed, things change. You can be that change.

Give up, or

Move on

So as an option to move on, I ask you to consider taking the same action that I have taken multiple times. Is it easy? No. Will it be emotional? Yes, very likely. It is an affordable solution to help you move forward. It offers you a chance to have your voice heard, to get some money, and restore your credit. It offers you a chance to get out from under a material thing -a house- that is likely killing you financially, and perhaps emotionally *and* putting strain on your family.

I hope you will join me by considering what I have proposed. It is not the *only* option. Surprisingly however, as I read and study practically everything I can get my hands on about the housing crisis-written by America's brightest financial minds- I do not see many other options offered.

We talked about other options in this book-expensive, time consuming options. Options that do not allow you to move forward for many years. If you have the money, and the heart, I strongly encourage you to fight in a higher court. If you can afford it, this option is very gratifying and empowering. But if that is not an option in *your* financial situation, I ask you to consider my alternative.

Give up, or

Move on

If your choice is to give up, I ask you to do it for *just a little while.* Grieve. Be enraged by it. Process what happened to you. Maybe even scream! And then **take action** so life can offer you option 2 and many more options 2's in the future.

Alan R. Sims

About the Author

Alan R. Sims is a nationally recognized expert on mortgage fraud and real estate related issues. In January, 2011 he assisted a homeowner in proving fraud against a large bank. It was the first verdict of its kind since the housing crisis began.

While not an attorney, he is consulted by attorneys nationwide as an expert witness to build cases against banking, mortgage firms, and mortgage scam operations. He teaches attorneys and judges in a California State Bar approved continuing education courses on real estate matters.

In 2009 he formed The Center for Litigation and Consumer Real Estate Education, a nonprofit, to empower homeowners to fight back against their banks and mortgage companies. Recently, the name has been changed to Courtroom Advocates.[38]

In 1993, Mr. Sims established Alan R. Sims: A Forensic Real Estate Appraisal Firm[39] after an extensive career as an engineer. Having a passion for helping "the little guy," he has collaborated on many a

---

[38]   http://Courtroom-Advocates.com

[39]   www.AlanSims.com

real estate battle and considers it a privilege to help others.

Ways to Contact the Author

Have questions? Comments?

I receive hundreds of telephone calls daily from all over the nation. **The best way** to reach me is by email. Also I invite you to make comments on social media. I would love to hear from you and answer your questions. Thank you for purchasing my book.

Depending on your court and the judge, you may not need to hire an expert. I am available if you require additional assistance. My fees are posted on my website. Helping you with your case will take me 3-4 hours depending on complexity. As a reminder, you can ask the judge to reimburse you for this expense.

Here are ways to contact me:

Email (best way to reach me)

* **AlanSims@Courtroom-Advocates.com**

Social Media

If you have comments about the book, I would love to hear them. This is the best place to post comments and suggestions.

- **Sue Your Bank-the book Facebook fan page:** search for "Sue Your Bank-the book"

- **Courtroom Advocates Twitter:** @CourtAdvocates

- **My personal Facebook profile page:** search for "Alan R. Sims."

- **Courtroom Advocates Facebook fan page: search for** "Courtroom Advocates."

- **YouTube Channel for Courtroom Advocates:** http://www.youtube.com/user/courtroomadvocates

Support Group

On Facebook, search for "Sue Your Bank Elite Support Group." [40]

---

[40] http://www.facebook.com/groups/470948546248862/

Description: This is a secret, members only Facebook support group where homeowners can learn from each other, share experiences, share what works and what does not, and have their questions answered. If you purchased this book, I invite you to join us on this site. I offer this as a thank you for purchasing my book.

Benefits:

- Access to ask Alan R. Sims your questions.

- Be the first to receive updates and announcements.

- Announcements on press appearances.

- Learn from other homeowners on experiences in the courtroom and tips they may have learned and would like to share.

To Gain Access:

- Search "Sue Your Bank Elite Support Group" and click "ask to join" at the top right side of the page. One of the page administrators will "let you in."

Alan R. Sims

Book Promotion

I am offering a chance to win a consultation with me if you purchased this book.

Please visit http://SueYourBank.com for more information on this promotion.

What you will win: I am giving away a consultation worth $450.00 with me to help you on your small claims court journey. This giveaway does not include court costs, proof of service to the defendant, skip trace services or incidentals. This offer includes 3-4 hours of my time via telephone to assist you. I will provide you with a written declaration to give to the judge when you make your case.

Alan R. Sims

Legal Vocabulary

All definitions are taken from Black's Law Dictionary, seventh edition. Some of the terms are mentioned in this book, while others are placed here for your information. *It is not expected that you memorize the definitions of each one.*

Affidavit: A voluntary declaration of facts, written down and sworn to be the declarant before an officer authorized to administer oaths.

Agent: One who is authorized to act for or in place of another.

Burden of Proof: A party's duty to prove a disputed assertion or charge.

Consideration: Something of value (such as an act, a forbearance, or a return promise) received by a promisor from a promisee. Consideration, or a substitute such as promissory estoppel, is necessary for an agreement to be enforceable.

Contract: (1) An agreement between two or more parties creating obligations that are enforceable or otherwise recognizable at law (a binding contract). (2) The writing that sets forth such an agreement (a contract is valid if valid under the law of the residence of the party wishing to enforce the contract).

Damages: Money claimed by, or ordered to to be paid to, a person as compensation for loss or injury.

Exemplary Damages: see *punitive damages*.

Punitive Damages: Damages awarded in addition to actual damages when the defendant acted with reckless, malice, or deceit. Punitive damages, which are intended to punish and thereby deter blameworthy conduct, are generally not recoverable for breach of contract. The Supreme Court held that three guidelines help determine whether a punitive damages award violates constitutional due process: (1) the reprehensibility of the conduct being punished; (2) the reasonableness of the relationship between the harm and the award; and (3) the difference between the award and the civil penalties authorized in comparable cases. Also termed exemplary damages; vindictive damages; punitory damages; presumptive damages; added damages; aggravated damages; speculative damages; imaginary damages; smart money; punies.

Reliance Damages: Damages awarded for losses incurred by the plaintiff in reliance on the contract.

Treble Damages: Damages that, by statute, are three times the amount that the fact finder (*the judge*) determines is owed. Also termed triple damages.

Deed in Lieu of Foreclosure: A deed by which a borrower conveys fee-simple title to a lender in satisfaction of a mortgage debt and as a substitute for foreclosure. This deed is often referred to simply as "deed in lieu."

Defendant: A person who is sued in a civil proceeding or accused in a criminal proceeding.

Detrimental Reliance: Reliance by one party on the acts or representations of another, causing a worsening of the first party's position. Detrimental reliance may serve as a substitute for consideration and thus make a promise enforceable as a contract. See *promissory estoppel*.

Estoppel: (1) A bar that prevents one from asserting a claim or right that contradicts what one has said or done before or what has been legally established as true. (2) A bar that prevents the relitigation of issues. (3) An affirmative defense alleging good-faith reliance on a misleading representation and an injury or detrimental change in position resulting from that reliance.

Equitable Estoppel: (1) defensive doctrine preventing one party from taking unfair advantage of another when, through false language or conduct, the person to be estopped has induced another person to act in a certain way, with the result that the other person has been injured in some way. This doctrine is founded on principles of fraud. The five essential elements for this type of estoppel are (a) that there was a false representation or concealment of material facts, (b) that the representation must have been known to be false by the party making it, or the party must have been negligent in not knowing its falsity, (c) that it was believed to be true by the person to whom it was mae, (d) that the party making the representation must have intended that it be acted on, or the person acting on it must have been justified in assuming this intent, and (e) that the party asserting estoppel acted on the representation in a way that will result in a substantial prejudice unless the claim of estoppel succeeds. Also termed *estoppel by* *conduct; estoppel in pais* (2) See *promissory estoppel.*

Promissory Estoppel: The principle that a promise made without consideration may nonetheless be enforced to prevent injustice if the promisor should have reasonably expected the promisee to rely on the promise and if the promisee did actually rely on the promise to his or her detriment. Also termed <u>inaccurately</u> *equitable estoppel.*

Exhibit: (1) A document, record, or other tangible object formally introduced as evidence in court.

Fraud: (1) A knowing misrepresentation of the truth or concealment of a material fact to induce another to act to his or her detriment. Fraud is usually a *tort*, but in some cases (especially when the conduct is willful) it may be a crime. (2) A misrepresentation made recklessly without belief in its truth to induce another person to act, (3) A tort arising from a knowing misrepresentation, concealment of material fact, or reckless misrepresentation made to induce another to act to his or her detriment. (4) Unconscionable dealing, especially in contract law, the unconscientious use of the power arising out of the parties' relative positions and resulting in an unconscionable bargain.

In the legal dictionary there are many specific types of fraud. I have included some definitions that may prove interesting to you and may be applicable to your particular situation:

Fraud in the Factum: Fraud occurring when a legal instrument (*such as a contract*) as actually executed differs from the one intended for execution by the person who executes it, or when the instrument may have had no legal existence. Compared to *fraud in the inducement, fraud in the factum* occurs only rarely, as when a blind person signs a mortgage when misleadingly told that it's just a letter (*also when English is their second language, for example*). Also termed *fraud in the execution; fraud in the making.* Compare to *fraud in the inducement.*

Fraud in the Inducement: Fraud occurring when a misrepresentation leads another to enter into a transaction with a false impression of the risks, duties, or obligations involved; an intentional misrepresentation of a material risk or duty reasonably relied on, thereby injuring the other party without vitiating the contract itself, especially, about a fact relating to value. Compare to *fraud in the factum.*

Promissory Fraud: A promise to perform made when the promisor had no intention of performing the promise. Also termed *common-law fraud.*

In Forma Pauperis: (also called fee waiver, IFP affidavit, pauper's affidavit, poverty affidavit). Latin for "in the manner of a pauper." In the manner of an indigent who is permitted to disregard filing fees and court costs. When suing, a poor person is generally entitled to proceed *in forma pauperis.*

Intentional Infliction of Emotional Distress: The tort of intentionally or recklessly causing another person severe emotional distress through one's extreme or outrageous acts. In a few jurisdictions, a physical manifestation of the mental suffering is required for the plaintiff to recover damages. (**Note:** *I mention this definition as one to consider if you life in a court with a high small claims limit or if you wish to go to a higher court. You may have to provide the testimony or declaration of the treating physician or therapist. Check your state's court rules*).

Jurisdiction: (1) A government's general power to exercise authority over all persons and things within its territory. (2) A court's power to decide a case or issue a decree. (3) A geographical area within a political or judicial authority may be exercised. (4) political or judicial subdivision within such an area. Also called *venue*.

Misrepresentation: (1) The act of making a false or misleading statement about something, usually with the intent to deceive. (2) The statement so made; an assertion that does not accord with the facts. Also termed *false representation* or *false misrepresentation*.

> **Fraudulent Misrepresentation:** A false statement that is known to be false or is made recklessly-without knowing or caring whether it is true or false-and that is intended to induce a party to detrimentally rely on it. Also terms *fraudulent representation; deceit.*

> **Material Misrepresentation:** In *contracts*: a false statement that is likely to induce a reasonable person to assent or that the maker knows is likely to induce the recipient to assent.

Plaintiff: The party who brings a civil suit in a court of law (the person who sues).

***Pro Tem* judge:** A visiting judge. A judge appointed by the presiding judge of an administrative region to sit temporarily on a given court., usually in the regular judge's absence. Also termed judge *pro tempore*.

Pro Se: Latin for oneself; on one's own behalf; without a lawyer. One who represents oneself in a court proceeding without the assistance of a lawyer. *A term usually used in Federal Court.*

Pro Per: Also called pro persona; sometimes shortened to pro per. For one's own person. On one's own behalf. *A term usually used in State Court.*

Reasonable Person: A hypothetical person used as a legal standard, especially to determine whether someone acted with negligence. The reasonable person acts sensibly, does things without serious delay, and takes proper but not excessive precautions.

Statute of Frauds: (1) An English statute enacted in 1677 declaring certain contracts judicially unenforceable (but not void) if they are not committed to writing and signed by the party to be charged. The statute was entitled "An Act for the Prevention of Frauds and Perjuries" - also termed Statute of Frauds and Perjuries. (2) A statute (based on the English Statute of Frauds) designed to prevent fraud and perjury be requiring certain contracts to be in writing and signed by the party to be charged. **Statute of frauds traditionally apply to the following types of contracts:**

- a contract for the sale or transfer in the interest of land (real estate).

- a contract that cannot be performed within one year of its making

- a contract for the sale of goods valued at $500 or more,

- a contract of an executor or administrator to answer for a decedent's debt,

- a contract to guarantee the debt or duty of another

- a contract made in consideration of marriage.

Tort: A civil wrong for which a remedy may be obtained, usually in the form of damages.

Undue Influence: (1) The improper use of power or trust in a way that deprives a person of free will and substantiates another's objective. (2) Consent to a contract, transaction, relationship, or conduct tis voidable if the consent is obtained through undue influence.

Unjust Enrichment: (1) The retention of a benefit conferred on another, without offering compensation, in circumstances where compensation is reasonably expected. (2) A benefit obtained from another, not intended as a gift and not legally justifiable, for which the beneficiary must make restitution or recompense. (3) The area of law dealing with unjustifiable benefits of this kind.

Alan R. Sims

Suggested Reading & Helpful Links
Information about Small Claims Court

FreeAdvice.com: http:// www.freeadvice.com/fa_google_search.php? cx=partner- pub-3387887484387515:ih042l-3ab7&cof=F ORID:9&ie=UTF-8&q=small+claims&sa=

Google Scholar for legal research. http:// scholar.google.com/schhp?hl=en

National Center for State Courts. You can search for information on your state's small claims court. http://www.ncsc.org

National Association of Consumer Advocates. NACA is a nationwide organization that represent people victimized by fraudulent, predatory, and abusive business practices. http://www.naca.net

NOLO Links on Small Claims Court:

Recommended Book: Everybody's Guide to Small Claims Court by Ralph Warner.

Small Claims Rules by State: As I stated earlier in this book, some of these links unfortunately lead no where as your state may have moved their court information to another site since this Nolo site was published. http://www.nolo.com/legal-encyclopedia/small-claims-court-in-your-state-31016.html

How Much to Sue for In a Contract Case: This site is to be used for a guideline and in addition to the information I provided you in this book. http://www.nolo.com/legal-encyclopedia/free-books/small-claims-book/chapter4-4.html

Multiple Links on Small Claims Court info: http://www.nolo.com/legal-encyclopedia/small-claims-court

How to Prepare for Your Day in Court: http://www.nolo.com/legal-encyclopedia/free-books/small-claims-book/chapter13-9.html

The Basics about Attorney's Fees: http://www.nolo.com/legal-encyclopedia/attorneys-fees-basics-30196.html

Small Claims Basic Information: This is very general information that will provide you with an overview. It is not specific to your state. http://www.nolo.com/legal-encyclopedia/free-books/small-claims-book/chapter1-1.html

Legal Research: http://www.nolo.com/legal-research

Statutes of Limitations in each state. This link is for Nolo.com. They do their best to see that the information is up to date. Be sure that the time limit on the statute of limitations has not changed since they published this link. http://www.nolo.com/legal-encyclopedia/statute-of-limitations-state-laws-chart-29941.html

50-State Chart of Small Claims Court Dollar Limits. This link is for Nolo.com. They do their best to see that the information is up to date. Be sure that the dollar amount has not changed since they published this link. It could have increased in your state since the publishing of this link. http://www.nolo.com/legal-encyclopedia/small-claims-suits-how-much-30031.html

Class Actions in Small Claims Court. This may be a link worth exploring. Many Americans have formed support groups. If all of you have the same issue, this may be an avenue to read more about. http:// www.nolo.com/legal-encyclopedia/free-books/small-claims-book/chapter7-12.html

Foreclosure Information

Defenses to Foreclosure. Challenging a foreclosure by bringing a defense such as unconscionability (unreasonable) or lender mistake. http://www.nolo.com/legal-encyclopedia/defenses-foreclosure-29937.html

How to Fight Foreclosure in Court. This is a partial summary of one of the issues covered in the book below. http:// www.nolo.com/legal-encyclopedia/how-fight-foreclosure-court-nonjudicial-foreclosure.html

The Foreclosure Survival Guide: Keep Your House or Walk Away With Money in Your Pocket by Stephen Elias. I advise you to invest in the most recent edition of this book. At the time of my book release the latest edition of Mr. Elias' book is the Third Edition

September 2011. I recommend this book because he helps you assess your situation honestly and arms you with the facts. He is honest about HAMP and how ineffective it is right now due to overwhelming amounts of homeowners applying to this program. It also offers advice in considering bankruptcy. Since I am not an attorney I do not feel comfortable giving you such advice, so I urge you to consult this book written by an attorney who knows. This book also explains foreclosure rescue scams which the majority of the clients I help have been victimized by. I also advise you to consult the back of the book for laws in your individual state. Mr. Elias is spot on as to what the scammers say to get you to hand over your money-and in many cases, hand over your house!

The bottom line is, if you cannot pay your mortgage, little can be done to avoid losing your home. The majority of these organizations-including some law firms (or organizations dressed to look like law firms) are just trying to make money off of you. Please educate yourself. This book is a great place to do that.

Triance Foreclosure Defenses: Non-Bankruptcy & Bankruptcy Remedies. The Essential Deskbook for the Consumer Law Professional by Craig Triance. These pricey books are written for law professionals but if you wanted to represent yourself, you may want to consult these books. They are used by many lawyers who specialize in this field. This is a book you may want to consult if you are going to a higher court and fighter broader issues.

Foreclosures: Defenses, Workouts, and Mortgage Servicing. Authored by the staff of the National Consumer Law Center, this is the best book out there for in-depth legal research on the subject of foreclosure. It covers how to negotiate pre-foreclosure workout agreements; current workout options with Fannie Mae, Freddie Mac, HUD, VA, and RHS; how to challenge mortgage servicer abuses; foreclosure litigation, including power of sale, due on sale, and substantive and procedural defenses; raising loan broker and loan originator-related claims against the mortgage holder; special rights to stop foreclosure of FHA, VA, and RHS mortgages; mobile home foreclosures; and tax liens and tax foreclosures. It comes with a CD that contains a lot of the forms, foreclosure laws, and other materials you will need if you want to fight a foreclosure or do your own workout with your lender. You can buy a copy for around $100, or perhaps find a copy in your local law or general-purpose library. This too is a book you may want to consult if you are going to a higher court and fighter broader issues. http://fcic.law.stanford.edu/report

Financial Crisis Inquiry Commission: This is the 600+ page report generated by the Federal Government that examines the causes of the financial and economic crisis as of January 2011. This commission was established as part of the Fraud Enforcement and Recovery Act passed by Congress and signed by the President in May 2009. http://fcic.law.stanford.edu/report

Low or No Cost Legal Help

National Assn. of Consumer Advocates. You may find some assistance and advice here. It is an organization of more than 1,500 attorneys who represent consumers victimized by fraudulent, abusive and predatory business practices. http://www.naca.net

Legal Services Corporation. They are the single largest funder of civil legal aid for low-income Americans in the nation. According to their website, more than 25% of cases involve helping to resolve landlord-tenant disputes, helping homeowners prevent foreclosures or renegotiate their loans, assisting renters with eviction notices whose landlords are being foreclosed on, and helping people maintain federal housing subsidies when appropriate. They oversee legal aid programs in your state-which I advise you to seek out. http://www.lsc.gov/about/what-is-lsc

LawHelp.org. Visit their website and click on your state. They assist low and moderate income families find free legal aid programs. http://www.lawhelp.org

Miscellaneous Links

Federal Reserve for information on Foreclosure Resource Centers. http://www.federalreserve.gov/consumerinfo/foreclosure.htm

Federal Trade Commission for consumer facts of foreclosure scams. http://www.ftc.gov/bcp/menus/consumer/credit/mortgage.shtm

Foreclosure Law: A website with information on your state's foreclosure laws. http://www.foreclosurelaw.org

Housing and Urban Development- "HUD" has a section on foreclosure issues. http://portal.hud.gov/hudportal/HUD?src=/topics/avoiding_foreclosure

Making Home Affordable-a federal government website that offers information on eligibility requirements for loan modifications. http://www.makinghomeaffordable.gov/pages/default.aspx

National Consumer Law Center-links on foreclosure, foreclosure scams, and predatory lending issues. Be sure to see their **foreclosure laws by states.** http://www.nclc.org/state-foreclosure-laws/

National Foundation for Credit Counseling-a directory of nonprofit credit counselors as well as housing counselors who can assist your with foreclosure issues. http://www.nfcc.org

Hardest Hit Fund-This program is available in 18 states at the time of this book publication. http://www.treasury.gov/ initiatives/financial-stability/programs/ housing-programs/hhf/Pages/default.aspx

Nolo's Bankruptcy Information. A website of general information. http:// www.nolo.com/legal-encyclopedia/content/ best-bankruptcy-websites.html

Suggested Books

Links to the following books can be found here: http://courtroom-advocates.com/ recommended-books

Nolo's Everybody's Guide to Small Claims Court by Ralph Warner

Getting to Yes: Negotiating without Giving In by Willam Ury and Roger Fisher

Getting Past No: Negotiating in Difficult Situations by William Ury

Nolo's Represent Yourself in Court: How to Prepare & Try a Winning Case by Paul Bergman and Sara Berman-Barrett.

The Housing Boom and Bust by Thomas Sowell

Help Other Homeowners & Make a Change

"We the people" have a loud voice when we all work together. It's how our nation was built.

For over 20 years I have been earning the trust of American property owners. I have dedicated my life to making changes. I wrote this book because it is my life's work to empower homeowners to fight back. The laws in our society are not made unless we speak up. The law "sits back" and waits for things to happen to us *and then* the laws are made. It usually does not work in reverse. Laws are also made when we take a stand and get the word out. When judges see the courts overrun with this type of complaint they start talking to each other, to their organizations, to their government leaders and changes are made.

No doubt you know the power of social media (Facebook, Twitter, YouTube, Pinterest, etc.). It has caught on because it is very democratic. These platforms amplify your voice by allowing you to recommend and review products. It is my hope that you will do this with this book. Press that "like" button and tweet!

There is so much misinformation and too few solutions regarding this issue. You can help other homeowners by writing a review of this book and writing a post on your social media platforms.

The more reviews this book has, the more attention it gets by other homeowners who are desperately search for answers-and you can provide them with your "voice."

Books sellers respond by promoting this book based on your reviews and clicks on the "like" button and makes it more visible in their search engines. This is exactly what makes the social media process a democratic one.

You can also **devastate the banks** when you leave a review because the more people that know about this book, the more homeowners are empowered to fight back. Real change occurs when we the people speak out. Writing a review is one way.

Legislation, such as H.A.M.P. is not working, however, your voice is louder than that. Your review can start a change. If you are reading this book from certain models of the Kindle (and other ebook readers), you will also have a chance to rate SUE YOUR BANK and share your rating of 1-5 stars with your friends on Facebook and Twitter at the very end of the book .

As someone who has served the public all my life, I am interested in what you have to say. I personally read all the reviews. If you have a moment, I would be grateful for your review. If you have question or comments I would love you to contact me by email and through the social media links I provided in this book (above).

Remember when *you* were looking for answers? Remember how difficult that was because hidden among the real answers were advertisements for scam after scam? Point other homeowners in the right direction to find answers with your book review, as well as on social media. I thank you in advance for this small action.

THANK YOU again for buying my book!

Alan R. Sims

¿Hablas español?

Demande a su Banco! will translated if funding permits in 2013. The Latin community has been decimated by the housing crisis. Spread the word!

Help the Spanish speaking community by volunteering to be an interpreter at your local court. Your services are needed!

26907976R00126

Made in the USA
Lexington, KY
21 October 2013